LEGIBILITY IN CHILDREN'S BOOKS

LEGIBILITY IN CHILDREN'S BOOKS

A Review of Research

Lynne Watts
and
John Nisbet

NFER Publishing Company Ltd.

Published by the NFER Publishing Company Ltd.,
Book Division, 2 Jennings Buildings, Thames Avenue,
Windsor, Berks., SL4 1QS
Registered Office, The Mere, Upton Park, Slough, Bucks., SL1 2DQ
First Published 1974
© Lynne Watts and John Nisbet
85633 034 5

Printed in Great Britain by
King, Thorne & Stace Ltd., School Road, Hove, Sussex, BN3 5JE
Distributed in the USA by Humanities Press Inc.
450 Park Avenue South, New York, N.Y. 10016, USA

74 - 189198

Contents

Acknowledgments

THIS REVIEW of research was sponsored and supported financially by W. and R. Chambers Ltd., educational publishers, Edinburgh. Mr I. Gould, Mrs A. Paterson, Miss G. Gould, Dr M. Clark, Dr W. B. Dockrell, Mr R. K. Duthie, Mr R. Fyfe and Miss M. Taylor are among the many persons whose assistance is gratefully acknowledged. The publishers wish to express their thanks to the Monotype Corporation for their permission to reproduce from *The Monotype Handbook* the illustration on page 28 and to W. and R. Chambers Ltd. for permission to reproduce material from *Enjoy Reading! Book I* (1967).

Introduction

THE ADULT READER takes for granted the legibility of print, though one has only to read an old text, or a badly printed page, to appreciate the achievements of modern printing. Typography is important for the child who is learning to read, who may be helped or hindered by type face, size of print, spacing and lay-out of the text. Of course, there are other considerations, possibly more important in aiding learning: the content and its effect on motivation; the level and range of vocabulary; the child's own background of experience, his attitudes and abilities; methods of teaching; and so on. In the research literature on reading, these other considerations have received most attention, whereas the extensive research on typography is not well known to teachers, nor even to publishers of children's books.

Consequently, our aim is to review research in the field of typography as it affects children's books, and to set it in the context of research on reading. Essentially, we are concerned with legibility. (Perhaps 'readability' would have been a better word to use, but it has been appropriated for a different use, with the advent of 'readability formulae'.) It is probably unnecessary to conduct experiments to prove that, at the extremes, legibility is important. For example, a child taught to read from the tiny print and minimal spacing of a pocket Bible will be handicapped by problems of legibility of the print. At the other extreme very large print with excessive use of spacing would provide an obstacle to the formation of effective reading skills. Within these two extremes, research studies have attempted to discover just how typography and lay-out affect an individual's ability to read a page of print, and in so doing, to set limits which provide the conditions for optimal legibility. For example, what are the limits set on length of line, or can a child learn to read equally well from long and short lines? Are certain typefaces easier to learn from than others? How important is the size of print and what is the optimum spacing between lines and between words? These are questions on which the publisher of children's books must make a decision. They are also questions that teachers and those responsible for the development of reading skills in children should understand when selecting books for the young reader.

It is important to emphasize that learning to read cannot be attributed to the action of one factor but must be viewed as a process in which all factors—child, teacher, method, content and typography—interact. Though it is convenient in research to isolate any one of these factors from the remainder, one must ultimately bring the various aspects together and consider their importance in the context of a single process. In this way the factor is placed in its correct perspective as one of the many interrelated factors involved in the complicated task of motivating and assisting a child to learn to read fluently.

SECTION ONE

Problems of Definition and Measurement

MOST OF US can read, but few of us have any conscious awareness of the underlying perceptual mechanism we employ to extract information from written material. Once we have mastered the initial problem of learning to read, the mechanical skills involved quickly become automatic and are applied without conscious effort.

A fluent reader reads at a rate of 250 to 300 words a minute. His eyes do not run smoothly along a line of print, but move in a series of small rapid jerks. The eye in reading a line of 90 mm. will pause approximately six to eight times, then will sweep back to begin the next line. It is only when the eye pauses that perception takes place. This is called a fixation pause and, under normal reading conditions, approximately 90 per cent of reading time is devoted to such pauses (Tinker 1965). Each lasts for approximately one-fiftieth of a second (Kerr, 1926) and the number of letters perceived during the fixation pause varies according to the size of print and the

Figure 1: *Fixation points in lines of reading*

2 1 3 4 6 5 7
The boys were playing on the beach when

1 2 3 4 5
suddenly Jim noticed something moving

1 2 4 3 5
in the water. He called to his brother

angle and distance of the text from the eye as well as to the skill and experience of the reader. A detailed account of these variations in the number of letters perceived is to be found in Carmichael and Dearborn (1972).

Sometimes the eyes make a backward movement, called a regression. This commonly occurs when the reader experiences difficulty in understanding the text, due to difficulties in comprehension or in perception. When a reader has little difficulty in comprehending or perceiving the written material, there will be relatively fewer regressions and fewer fixation pauses of a shorter duration.

Primarily, the measurement of legibility under experimental conditions has been based on measurement of one (or more) aspects of the mechanical process involved in reading. Where the content of the printed material is either meaningless (as in the case of non-sense syllables) or well below the threshold of normal adult comprehension, the obtained measurements should reflect differences due to the ease of perception, unconfounded by problems of comprehension. It is of course open to question whether this is a valid measure of reading, a point which is discussed in more detail later in this section.

In the research literature there has been a lengthy debate as to which particular aspect of the mechanical skill of reading affords the best measurement of legibility. The heart of the problem lies in the concept of 'legibility'. Differences in interpretation of this word have led to wide divergences of opinion as to the most appropriate criterion for its measurement. No one single method has a clear advantage over others; and while some methods correlate highly with one another, others produce conflicting results.

The most commonly used definition of legibility (suggested by Ovink, 1938) refers to *the ease and accuracy with which a reader is able to perceive the printed word*.

Pyke (1926) criticizes the use of the word 'ease' in a definition of legibility, pointing out that 'it does not follow, because you read accurately, or rapidly, or both, that you do so without effort . . . or without eye strain or fatigue'. Pyke based his definition of legibility on the criteria of accuracy and speed of reading running text. Luckiesh and Moss (1940) are concerned with the 'visibility' or visual acuity of printed material and a measure of legibility that denotes 'ease of seeing when applied to the performance of the specific task of reading'. Tinker (1965) uses, among other criteria, reader's opinions as a measure of legibility. Zachrisson (1965), who is concerned with the meaningful interpretation of a text, defines legibility 'as the speed and accuracy of visually receiving and comprehending meaningful running text'. The following references contain detailed discussions of the problems encountered by researchers in both defining and in measuring legibility: Pyke (1926); Tinker (1963); Zachrisson (1965); and Carmichael and Dearborn (1972).

The various measures of legibility used in research studies, can be divided into two broad groups:

  i. those which use criteria that can be measured objectively and with a high degree of accuracy; and

  ii. more subjective measures of legibility which use criteria that represent a broader concept of legibility.

The objective, or quantitative methods of measurement can be classified as measures of functional criteria (Zachrisson, 1965). Examples are:

  i. distance of perception—measures of visual material at varying distances;

  ii. speed of perception—timed exposure of material, as presented by a *tachistoscope*, an instrument which permits perception under controlled conditions;

  iii. peripheral vision, i.e. width of eye span;

  iv. visibility measures—illumination thresholds as measured by a tachistoscope;

  v. binocular rivalry—focus threshold;

  vi. Eye movements—oculomotor patterns as measured by a specifically designed camera. These include measures of:

    a. number and duration of eye pauses per line;

    b. number of regressions;

    c. regularity of eye movements;

vii. frequency of eye blinks;
viii. number of errors in comprehension or perception of printed
     material—usually presented by a tachistoscopic device.

Contrasted to these measures of legibility are the highly
qualitative and subjective measures of legibility that concern themselves with:

  i. observation of the subject for symptoms of fatigue and eye
     strain; and
 ii. subject opinions as to the pleasantness and legibility of the
     experimental material.

These criteria are used more normally in combination with more
objective measures of legibility. They have the advantage of providing a measure of the psychological factors that may affect legibility of
printed material.

The major criticism directed against many of the measures
listed above, is that measurement does not take place under *normal
reading conditions*. This criticism is particularly applicable to
measures based on short exposure techniques where eye movements *cannot* function normally. It is unlikely that any experimental
situation can measure under normal reading conditions. However,
experiments have been designed in an attempt to gain an accurate
measure of reading behaviour. The two most frequently used
methods are:

  i. rate of reading of a passage of continuous prose, where the speed
     of reading is measured and comprehension controlled by means
     of a post test;
 ii. 'rate of work', as devised by Tinker, where speed of reading is
     measured and comprehension controlled by writing in missing
     words in consecutive phrases. The difficulty of material is well
     below the comprehension threshold of the normal adult reader.

However, even when the measures are applied under conditions
described as being normal to the reading situation, there exists a
running controversy, where a distinction is made between 'decoding'
(identification of the printed symbols) and 'reading for comprehension'. Where the measurement is based on the reading of meaningful
material, and the results are controlled for comprehension, subjects

are regarded as having 'read' the text only when a predetermined level of comprehension of the material has been reached. The opposite argument is that, for an adequate measure of legibility, material need not be understood, provided that the words are identified.

The dilemma is a real one. On the one hand, for experimental purposes, it is clearly advantageous to distinguish perceptual factors from those involved in comprehension. The factor of comprehension introduces complicating considerations such as the level of difficulty of the content of the material and the intelligence of the reader. However, most teachers and psychologists would argue that to attempt to separate perception from comprehension is to miss the whole point of reading.

Results obtained from so-called 'pure' measures of perception have, in isolation, little relevance to the reading situation. At first sight it may seem that young children must be preoccupied with the perception of letters and individual word shapes. However, many psychologists argue that in the early reading situation word identification and the comprehension of material should not be separated as distinct tasks and that comprehension should be given priority over any consideration of precise decoding skills or of reading for speed. (This is the basis of the controversy over the 'look and say' versus 'phonic' methods of teaching young children to read.)

The purpose of this section has been to draw attention to the problems involved in arriving at a precise definition of legibility and to outline the controversy that exists between exponents of different methods of measurement. Unfortunately, many of the experiments on legibility have produced conflicting results. The explanation for this is to be found in the differing interpretations of legibility and the consequent differences in the methods of measurement.

The Reading Process

FOR THE STUDIES on legibility to be viewed in their correct perspective it is necessary to have some understanding of the nature of the reading situation as experienced by young children learning to read. The demarcation between the strategies used by the beginning reader as opposed to the fluent reader is emphasized by most researchers. Tinker (1963) found that children between the ages of 9 and 13 reacted to optimal typography conditions in a similar way to adults. His conclusions were based on the stabilization of oculomotor patterns: an objective measure of eye movements while reading. Buswell (1937) recorded similar results which were later verified by Ballantine (1951). Smith, in his book *Understanding Reading* (1971), gives an informative account of the reading process. He describes the development in strategies from beginning to fluent reading, as a gradation from 'mediated word identification' to 'immediate comprehension'. Smith is also in agreement with Tinker as to the age when the transition from one stage to the other more normally occurs. Owing to the wide range of individual differences, a generalization of this nature presupposes that there exist many children well beyond the age of nine or ten who do not possess fluent reading strategies and also many children (some as young as four or five) who possess the fluent reading strategies of an adult. If, then, the focus of our interest is on the young reader, these findings indicate that we are concerned with an age range from about five to ten years. The importance of establishing these age limits is that the factors affecting legibility in this age range may be very different from those applicable to adults or older children.

There are many aspects of learning to read. Smith (1971)

lists four: perceptual, linguistic, cognitive and motivational. To appreciate the complexity of the reading process, one must not only consider these four aspects, but also the relative role each plays in helping a child learn to read. Whether success in learning to read is a matter of motivation or 'reading readiness' (based on measures of cognitive, perceptual and linguistic skills) is a question that remains largely unanswered. Clark and Milne (1972) state 'that learning to read should not be regarded as a hierarchy of skills from lower to higher order, but as a developmental language process where the approaches in the initial stages will colour the children's motivation and their perception of reading as a purposeful and valuable activity'. Thus, to be able and to be willing to read are of equal importance.

It is possible to distinguish three stages in the process of learning to read. These are:

  i. dependency on visual information, such as illustrations;
 ii. the need to discriminate between letter and word forms and to categorize their distinctive features;
iii. the development of phrase reading, working towards the development of fluent reading strategies.

A child comes into the reading situation with linguistic and cognitive skills which will equip him to undertake the task of learning to read. He also has certain attitudes and expectations that may greatly influence his motivation and consequently the progress made. It is the child's objective to extract information from the written text. Goodman (1967) suggests that a fluent reader uses many types of cues to identify meaning and that there exist in any word more cues than he requires for its recognition. These cues may be gained from *particular letters* (especially first letters), the form or *shape of the word*, or they may be gained from the *meaning of the sentence*. Bicmiller (1970) suggests, from results obtained with 42 first-grade children, that the high percentage of reading errors based on contextual information, represents an attempt by the children to avoid using graphic information as much as possible. Therefore we can say, for both the beginning and the fluent reader, reading is partly what he sees and partly what he expects to see. The more difficulty a reader has with understanding the text, the more he may rely on graphic detail. Whether this is especially so in the case of the child learning to read remains open to question.

The implications of the stages towards the development of fluent reading skills, are not limited to considerations of content only. They are relevant also to the print and layout used in children's books. For example, children will find it difficult to discriminate between letters, when a typeface is used that emphasizes the similarities between letter forms. A typeface that emphasizes the 'invariant' features of letters and gives greater contrast in word form, would assist children in differentiating between letters and words. Examples of two typefaces with highly differentiated letter forms are Gill Medium and Modern 7 (see Figures 25 and 26).

Figure 2: *Typefaces emphasizing the differences and the similarities between letters (Perpetua and Univers)*

Sammy loved to be busy. He was never happier than when he was chuff-chuffing out of Derry Station on another trip to Uptown.

Three miles out of Derry the track climbed a steep hill, but Sammy knew how to take this part of the journey. 'Steady-and-slow!' he

Sammy loved to be busy. He was never happier than when he was chuff-chuffing out of Derry Station on another trip to Uptown.

Three miles out of Derry the track climbed a steep hill, but Sammy knew how to take

The ultimate aim is to learn to develop a full range of reading skills and to apply these where appropriate. All aspects of helping children to read should be directed towards this goal. Many books written for young readers may be doing much to hinder the development of fluent reading strategies, by restricting content and using excessively short phrases. Writers have concentrated on these methods in an attempt to lessen the heavy burden that is placed on a young reader's memory and attention span in the initial stages of learning to read. Bamberger (1972) connects the progress made in reading to the number of books read during a given period. He found 'that children do not read books because they cannot read, and they cannot read because they do not read books'.

Without experiencing the 'practical effect' of a great many children's books, training in reading skills *alone* will not produce fluent readers. Bamberger (1972) and Clark and Milne (1972) agree that the roles of the book and teacher are overestimated in the task of learning to read, and that the potential of other materials (such as comics, magazines, newspapers, etc.) and alternative media, is greatly undervalued.

In conclusion, it may be suggested that the publisher's task, in relation to the reading process as experienced by young children, is twofold:

i. to adopt typographic layouts that will facilitate speed reading and the development of 'immediate comprehension' of the written text;

ii. to provide reading material that will motivate a child to read the necessary number of books to make him a fluent reader.

Typographic Factors

SHAW (1969) lists three factors that affect legibility:

  i. printing characteristics;
 ii. reader characteristics;
iii. factors linking the reader and the print.

Number (iii) remains outside the influence of the publisher. It includes such factors as illumination of the printed material, the distance the material is held from the reader and the angle at which the material is held. Any material read under conditions of poor lighting, at a distance greater than the normal reading distance (approx. 14 inches) or at an angle greater than 45 degrees, will be more difficult to read than it would be under conditions providing for optimal legibility.

Reader characteristics include the physiological and psychological peculiarities of the reader, i.e. what he is able to see and what he wants to see. The publisher can provide for the more general of these characteristics, e.g. printing books suited to the average levels of perceptual development, meeting the tastes of young readers by printing adventure and mystery stories and providing colourful illustrations. It is difficult for the publisher to cater for the child who has an abnormal characteristic, e.g. astigmatism, myopia, etc.

Quite obviously the publisher's greatest sphere of influence is in the typographic layout of the books he prints. *Every decision the publisher makes affects legibility*. This is as true for the use of colour and illustrations as it is for decisions regarding the actual type. Decisions to be made include:

  i. the use of upper or lower case print;
 ii. the type face and the use of serifs;

iii. the size of type, the spacing between the lines, the length of the line and the boldness of the print;

iv. the size of margins and the use of justified or unjustified composition;

v. the thickness and nature of the paper surface to be used for printing;

vi. the use of colour both in print and in illustrations.

The above list is not exhaustive. It merely serves as an introduction to the criteria research studies have selected as a means of providing for optimal standards of legibility in children's books.

For the purposes of clarity, it has been necessary to isolate the research findings on legibility from the factors that confound their different application to the printing of children's books. The standards of legibility listed in this report are not meant as a list of rules to be followed rigidly by designers and printers. Instead they are intended to indicate the specific results of research studies, and should be used as a basis for decision-making in the same way as the cost, potential circulation or purpose of a book affects its publication.

Legibility as a priority may often suffer; but by knowing precisely what diminishes legibility, the designer is in a better position to decide how far reading efficiency should be reduced for considerations of impact, visual experience, 'atmosphere', etc. Spencer (1969) describes the designer as being in a better position to 'avoid fruitless innovation'. More importantly, legibility should not be needlessly sacrificed—if blue type is more legible than red, it costs no more to print and is artistically acceptable, then it would be foolish to choose the red in preference to blue. 'Congeniality' (a term used by Zachrisson to describe the aesthetic qualities attributed to print) and legibility need not be in opposition.

Upper and lower case print

The results of research studies into the relative legibility of upper case (capital letters) over lower case print can be summarized as follows.

i. Lower case print is read faster and is preferred more by fluent readers than is upper case.

Figure 3: *Setting in upper case only and in upper and lower case*

THE BRIGHT RED BUS HAD JUST STOP-
PED OUTSIDE THE SCHOOL, AND ALL
THE CHILDREN HAD NOISILY CLAM-
BERED OUT. AS HE WAS ABOUT TO
RING THE BELL FOR THE DRIVER TO
START, THE CONDUCTOR SPIED SOME-
THING LYING ON THE FLOOR OF THE
BUS.

The bright red bus had just stopped outside the
school, and all the children had noisily clambered
out. As he was about to ring the bell for the driver
to start, the conductor spied something lying on
the floor of the bus.

ii. The slow, meticulous reading found with beginner readers,
shows no differences between upper and lower case in speed
reading tests.

iii. Upper case letters are more legible than lower case when isolated
or contained in nonsense syllables.

iv. The poorer legibility of individual lower case letters is eliminated
when the letter is contained in a word. Thus, *n* is not confused
with *u* when placed in the word *hen*.

v. Beginners tend to use the first letter of a word, then its last
letter and finally its overall shape when relying on graphic
cues for word recognition.

vi. The overall shape of the word is not used as a cue to differentiate between words printed in capitals, to the same
extent as it is for words printed in lower case.

Tinker (1959) states that 'all capital print is difficult to read'. This is not the case for children. Research studies have shown that children are more familiar with capital letters than with lower case letters. They are able to name correctly more capital letters than lower case, to perceive capitals more easily and to experience less confusion in differentiating between individual letters.

This disagreement in research findings is due partly to the use of different measures of legibility. Tinker and those researchers who agree in finding that lower case print has greater legibility, have used speed of reading under 'normal reading conditions' as the criterion against which to measure legibility. These measures have failed to find any differences between the two types of print when using children as subjects. The studies which have isolated individual letters or used nonsense syllables as material, have found capital letters to be more legible than lower case. Legibility has been measured by matching procedures or under different conditions of exposure (e.g. distance, time, illumination). The poorer legibility of lower case letters disappears once the isolated units are put together in meaningful words.

In the same way that Tinker's findings with adults cannot be generalized to include children, the poorer legibility of lower case letters found in these studies cannot be generalized to the normal reading situation. The results obtained from attempts to measure responses in the normal reading situation are not in direct conflict with the findings from laboratory experiments. The two methods used refer to two different aspects of the reading situation. Tinker, for example, is concerned with reading for speed, while other researchers have been concerned with the child's ability to discriminate between letter and word forms. Each can provide a valid contribution to the study of legibility.

Tinker (1963) states categorically that lower case print is read more quickly and preferred by adults to similar material set in capital letters. Adults' speed of reading increased by 10 per cent when material was read in lower case print over a short period of time (approximately three-and-a-quarter minutes.) For a reading time of 20 minutes the retarding effect of material printed in capitals was 14 per cent. Ninety per cent of adults taking part in the study preferred reading the material printed in lower case to that in capitals. In a subsequent paper, Tinker (1965) suggests two reasons why material printed in capital letters hinders rapid reading.

  i. Capitals are read letter by letter and adults read by word unity.

  ii. The text in capitals covers 35 per cent more surface area than the same material in lower case, making eye scanning movements difficult.

For example, in relation to (i), Tinker (1965) suggests that the distinctive shape of words printed in lower case, as opposed to capitals, enables a word to be recognised as a whole and not letter by letter.

Figure 4: *The shape of words*

Where speed of reading is an important aim for young readers it would appear from Tinker's studies that lower case print would greatly enhance the development of fluent reading skills. On the other hand, it may be claimed that young children are not concerned with rapid reading but with the discrimination of letter and word forms.

The case is put by Webster (1965) that capital letters can be perceived at a greater distance than lower case and under poorer conditions of visibility (as measured by tachistoscopic exposures). It is questionable whether such measures of legibility are relevant to the reading situation, especially in the case of distance, a point which is made by Shaw (1969 p.26) when discussing the relative advantages of the different criteria used by researchers to measure legibility. Webster suggests that words such as 'dog', 'bog', 'god', 'gob', 'bop' printed in lower case cause a great deal of confusion. To the young reader, where reversal and inversion of word and letter forms are very common, these words appear very similar. The same words printed in all capitals have more distinctive letter forms, e.g. DOG, BOG, GOD, GOB, BOP. He attributes the differences in confusion between the two types of print to word recognition taking place only partially as a result of up-and-down letter outline. Of equal or greater significance is *letter sequence*. For example, where the word shape is the same, but sequence wrong, adults will recognize the error, as in 'rec*i*ept'; 'cat, act'. By using capital letters a child is helped to focus on individual letters and so become aware of sequence. This is especially important in special cases of reading handicap such as dyslexia where there is a need to train the eye to move from left to right.

A study by Williams, Blumberg and Williams (1970) is of particular significance here. Williams *et al.* found that while kindergarten children (non-readers) showed no consistent use of cue selectors for the recognition of nonsense syllables, first-graders (beginning readers) used the first letter most frequently as a cue and the last letter less frequently. They very seldom used overall shape as a cue. This is in contrast to the adults in the study (proficient readers) who, amongst a variety of strategies, used shape as a cue for recognition. Williams' study would support Webster's hypothesis regarding letter sequence as an important cue for adult readers in word recognition, but it would limit any generalization of this strategy to the beginning reader.

Smythe *et al.* (1971) found that kindergarten and first-grade children (five and six years) were able to recognize capital letters better than lower case, but by the end of grade two these differences had disappeared. Of the 26 capitals, only seven (C, G, M, N, P, Q and Z) were not discriminated correctly by at least 98 per cent of five-year-olds in kindergarten. The mean rate of correct identification for all capital letters was also 98 per cent for this age group. In contrast to capitals, the lower case letters show a wider range of ability to discriminate. Only 61 per cent of five-year-olds could discriminate between d and p but 100 per cent could successfully discriminate letters a, e, f, s, y. Some lower case letters were still giving difficulty at the end of grade two. These were b, d, p, q.

By means of factor analysis, Smythe *et al.* were able to suggest that different processes may be operating during the learning of capital and lower case letter names. For example, the naming of capital letters was related to the traditional sequence of the alphabet and to the frequency with which letters are used in printed text. On the other hand the ability to name a lower case letter depended on its relative legibility. These findings may merely reflect particular teaching methods or they may have greater significance by suggesting the possibility of an index of relative difficulty in learning capital and lower case letters.

Spencer (1969) gives a comprehensive account of the relative legibility of lower case and all capital print. Included are studies by Cattell, Sandford, Roethlein, Vernon, Ovink, Burt, Cohn, Ruben-camp, Pyke and Tinker. The results of three individual studies shall be included in this report to illustrate three different methods used by researchers to categorize the varying legibility of lower case letters.

Tinker (1928) summarized the research on legibility of lower case letters. He found the correlation between individual studies high, ranging from ·48 to ·88. Consistent trends throughout the seven studies were:

   i. letters of high legibility—d, m, p, q, w;
  ii. letters of medium legibility—j, r, u, x, y;
 iii. letters of low legibility—c, e, i, n, l.

He found little agreement between ten studies concerned with relative legibility of capital letters. A and L were generally regarded as high in legibility, while B–R, G–C and Q–O were often confused.

Smith (1928) graded letters into categories representing the difficulty they present to the reader. For example of those tested 30 per cent had difficulty discriminating b, p, q, d; 13 per cent had difficulty with r, h, f, i, j, m; about six per cent with e, u, x, y, t, z, l, and less than four per cent with a, c, w, o, m, s, g.

Dunn Rankin (1968) on the basis of experimental evidence, divided lower case letters into groups where confusion most often occurred. The groups were: e, a, s, c, o / n, u, m, w / b, p, d / h, f, l, k, c.

(Letters j, q, u, x and z were not included in his study because of their infrequent use in pre-primary and primary readers.)

Hodge (1962) attributed differences in legibility between lower case letters and capitals to the relative lack of critical detail in lower case letters. Reference to the groups of letters in the three studies described above should illustrate this point. Gibson *et al.* (1962) studying the developmental changes that occur between the ages of four and eight years, give some clues as to why children have difficulty in discriminating between certain letter forms.

At age four, for example, children can generally distinguish between an open shape and a closed shape (see 1 in Figure 1), or between a joined pattern and one which has a break in it (2). They are liable to have difficulty in recognizing the difference when a shape undergoes rotation and reversal (3), when a line is changed to a curve (4), or when a shape is distorted as it would be if seen from a different perspective. These changes are called 'transformations': the letters c and e illustrate 'break and close'; d, b, p, q, or m, w, illustrate 'rotation and reversal'.

Between ages four and eight, the capacity to make these discriminations improves, as is shown by the downward slope of the error curves in Figure 2. However, the slopes of the error curves are different, indicating that some of the discriminations are harder than others. Thus, there were few errors in 'break and close' at age four, and these errors dropped to nearly zero at age eight. Errors for 'perspective' were numerous at four, five and six, and were still numerous at eight. Errors for 'rotation and reversal' started high but dropped to nearly zero at eight. Errors for changes from line to curve were relatively high at age four, but showed a rapid drop at ages seven and eight.

Gibson's work is important in that it gives an insight into the difficulties that confront a young reader in the task of discriminating between letter forms. It points to the existence of critical features contained in a letter that assist in this discrimination process. Finally it suggests methods whereby letters may be more easily distinguished. For example, the break and close transformation between 'c' and 'e' can be emphasized by enclosing a larger area of white space within the 'e'.

Figure 5: *Examples of transformations*

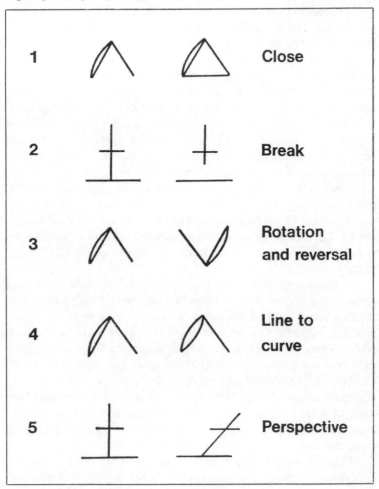

Research studies on the whole have recommended the use of lower case print in children's books (e.g. Huey, 1908; Burt, 1959; Tinker, 1965; Vernon 1971). The recommendations have been based on criteria measured with adults and consequently may not be

Figure 6: *Error curves showing rate of improvement in discriminating four types of transformation*

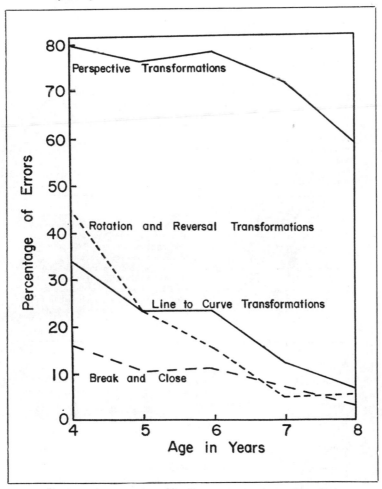

applicable to the young child learning to read. However, if speed of reading and immediate comprehension are to be the goals pursued by young readers, then a print that professes to emphasize these skills

Figure 7

The main typeface groups

Venetians and Old faces

These two groups display features which
show the calligraphic origin of lower-case
letter forms: the stress is diagonal and
serifs are bracketed and (except at the foot
of descenders) similarly slanted. In some
faces the diagonally sheared-off foot of b
is omitted altogether. Capitals are usually
somewhat shorter than ascenders. In the
Venetian faces (which preceded the true
Old faces) the bar of e is sloped in
harmony with stress and serif.

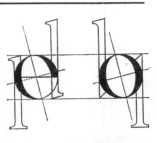

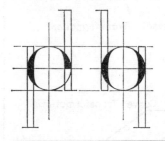

Modern faces

In the Modern faces most of the traces
of pen-made stress have disappeared:
shading is vertical serifs horizontal and
bracketing very fine or absent.
The contrast between thick and thin
strokes has increased. New features are
the double-curved tail of R and a foot
serif to b (a feature quite unnatural to
calligraphy). Capitals are usually the
full height of ascenders.

Transitional faces

During the 18th century, when the ideas
underlying the development of the Modern
face began to germinate, stress and serif
forms were gradually modified. The angle
of stress and serif was reduced and the
bracketing became finer. Individual letter
forms were modified and Modern forms
appeared side by side with Old-face forms.
The scythe-tailed Q used by Baskerville
became fashionable in England at this time.

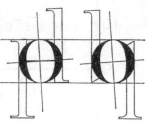

This figure © The Monotype Corporation

may be preferable to one that would possibly hinder their development. The lower legibility of many lower case letters can be minimized by using a typeface (e.g. Gill Medium) that emphasizes the differences between letters rather than their similarities.

Typeface and the use of serifs

The 'typeface' refers to the printing surface of the metal type. It also refers to the design or style of type. Zachrisson (1965) lists 19 typefaces in common use in Western Europe today. Each typeface can be classified as either *old face*, *transitional* or *modern* (see Figure 7) and may be printed in varying degrees of heaviness (or 'weight') e.g. bold, medium and light. The letters may have small finishing strokes at the top and bottom called *serifs* or they may be printed without these finishing strokes (*sans serif*). Each typeface has its own set of capitals, lower case, small capitals, italics, numbers and punctuation marks. This is known as the *fount* (or font).

From the results of empirical studies it is possible to list the factors of design that affect the legibility of a typeface. They include:

Figure 8: *Serif and sans-serif typefaces*

i. *The relative weight of thick and thin strokes*

Shading helps to differentiate between some letters (e.g. X and Z) but a *marked contrast* between thick and thin strokes does not contribute to legibility (Spencer, 1969). Burt (1959) found that the tendency to combine thick vertical strokes and thin curved and slanted strokes, diminished legibility when carried to extremes. The tendency for publishers to favour a sans serif typeface with uniform stroke and curve width is also criticized by Burt. He maintains that the 'rhythmic structure' of each printed word arises out of variation from thick to thin, and a uniform stroke of curve deprives the young reader of this feature of the pattern. Burt's assumption

Figure 9: *Typefaces with enclosed white space, hairlines and long and short ascenders and descenders*

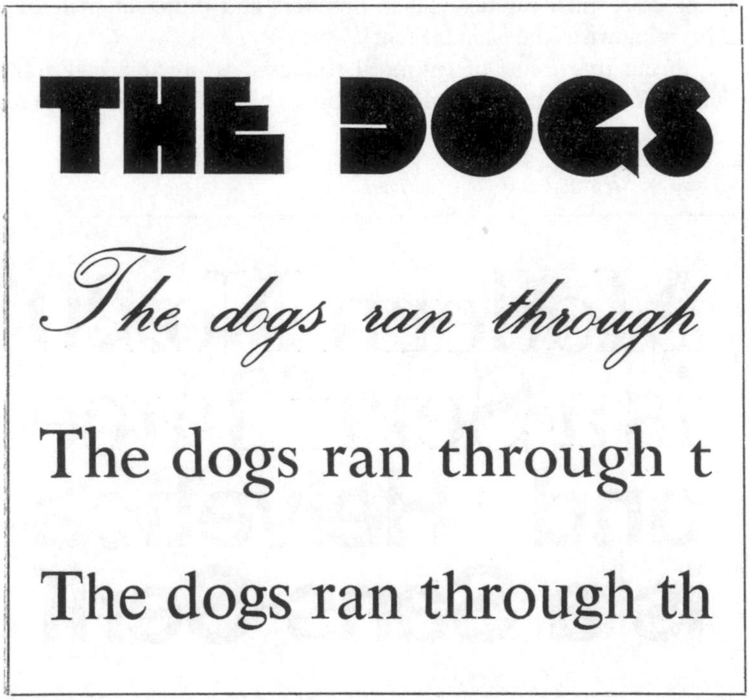

that 'old oblique shading is not only pleasanter to the eye, but easier to read' is based on an experiment carried out with adult readers. A modern sans serif typeface was not included in the sample of 19 old and modern typefaces which were studied in this experiment.

ii. *Relative area of white space enclosed within a letter*
It has been found (by tachistoscopic measurements) that the greater the relative area of the enclosed space within a letter, the greater its legibility (Burt, 1959; Tinker, 1965; Spencer, 1969.) Characteristics which might be thought helpful to legibility, may prove to have the opposite effect because they sometimes decrease the area of this enclosed space, such as the use of bold print, stress on curves, and the use of serifs and hairlines.

iii. *The length of ascenders and descenders in lower case print*
Longer ascenders and descenders (the parts of a letter which extend up or down) help to distinguish between letter and word forms by giving a distinctive shape to the letter or word. The eye tends to move along the top coastline of a line of print, picking up clues from the shape of the letters, to aid word recognition. This phenomenon has been used by Pitman in the development of i.t.a. where the distinguishing characteristics of augmented letters appear on the bottom of the letter. By using this method (as well as additional strokes within letters) Pitman (1961) maintains that interference with the recognition of the conventional letters of the alphabet is kept to a minimum, thus facilitating the changeover to traditional orthography.

Burt (1959) notes that while the long ascenders and descenders adopted by most modern faces tend to increase legibility of the isolated letters for younger children, they spoil the characteristic unity of the words for older readers. It is also necessary to consider this aspect of increasing legibility along with the spacing between lines ('leading') since the lines must be sufficiently distinct to provide a clear route for the eye to run along. Typefaces may increase legibility without demanding extra space by lengthening ascenders of letters and shortening descenders. In this way, space (an important cost factor) is not sacrificed for increased legibility.

Figure 10: *Initial teaching alphabet (i.t.a.)*

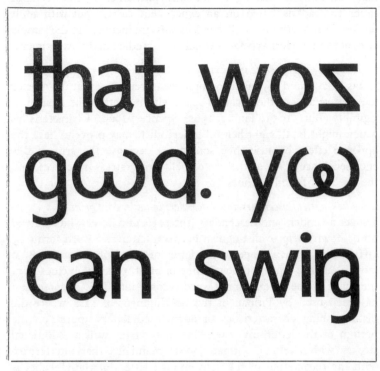

iv. *The use of serifs*

Burt (1959) claims that the use of serifs increases legibility by *distinguishing between similar letters, correcting for effects of irradiation*[1] and *aiding the horizontal movement of the eye* by 'combining separate letters into distinctive word wholes'. Burt, who is a strong advocate for the use of serifs in print, develops his argument in considerable detail in his book *A Psychological Study of Typography*. Unfortunately many of the opinions expressed are not substantiated by empirical evidence.

[1]'Irradiation' is the apparent extension of edges of an illuminated object as seen against a dark ground. A bright point appears bigger than reality, while a dark point appears smaller.

Prince (1967) devised a number of criteria for optimum legibility of print, based on relative degrees of visual acuity (as measured by a tachistoscope). He found letters without serifs to be more legible when read in isolation or in nonsense syllables than letters with serifs. The higher legibility of sans serif over serif letters applied even when a commonly used typeface such as Baskerville was compared to a less conventional sans serif typeface such as Spartan. However, when letters were combined into familiar words and made into sentences, the serif typeface was read more easily than the sans serif type. Prince attributes this increase in the legibility of serif type to the matching of the print to a picture image in the mind of the adult reader. Thus the *familiarity* of a serif typeface influenced its legibility when read in a conventional form. Prince maintains that for the young and the visually handicapped reader, who have no long established word-picture image developed, then a sans serif typeface will provide higher standards of legibility.

On the whole, the arguments opposing the use of serifs in books printed for very young readers, are based on the development of writing skills, rather than on any consideration of legibility. Teachers maintain that, to provide for maximum transfer between the two skills of reading and writing, letter forms should be the same for both. This also applies to a child imitating letters 'without thick and thin' in his handwriting (Burt 1959).

v. *Overall design of typeface*
The geometric design of modern typefaces is appreciated by many designers for its clarity and symmetry. However *clarity and legibility may be in conflict*. Modern typefaces are criticized for their tendency to accentuate the similarities between letters. A typeface that a teacher chooses for its clarity, absence of serifs and aesthetic qualities of symmetry, may present problems to the child who finds difficulty in discriminating between letter or word forms. Also a typeface which avoids extremes in the width of a letter, relative to its height has greater legibility. Prince (1967) suggests that 'letters without serifs, and having a width of not less than 80 per cent of their height, using the lower case "o" as the base dimension' have

B

Figure 11: *Condensed (Scotch Roman), average (Plantin) and broad (Perpetua)*
         typefaces

The bright red bus had just stopped outside the school, and all the children had
noisily clambered out. As he was about to
ring the bell for the driver to start, the
conductor spied something lying on the
floor of the bus.

The bright red bus had just stopped outside the school, and all the children had
noisily clambered out. As he was about to
ring the bell for the driver to start, the
conductor spied something lying on the
floor of the bus.

The bright red bus had just stopped outside the
school, and all the children had noisily clambered
out. As he was about to ring the bell for the
driver to start, the conductor spied something
lying on the floor of the bus.

the greatest legibility. Alternatively Burt (1959) states that 'condensed faces tend to look blurred to the hypermetropic eye while excessively expanded faces tend to disrupt the word form.'

Although it is possible to list factors that affect the legibility of a typeface, it is difficult to relate these factors specifically to the type of print to be used in books for the young reader. No study of legibility of typeface which uses children as subjects, has been found. The inferences made by many researchers regarding the legibility of different typefaces for use in children's books, have been based on:

  i. legibility studies carried out with adults or older children (10–11 years in the case of Burt);
 ii. their ideas of what is involved in the process of learning to read;
iii. the relationship between writing and reading skills. (This last consideration is not strictly a matter of legibility, although it may influence a teacher's opinion of what constitutes a 'legible' typeface.)

Researchers on the whole substantiate their argument by reference to these three points. Tinker (1959), when referring specifically to typeface, made the following blanket statement: 'The results of studies of adult reading should be applicable to printing for children'. Tinker fails to qualify this statement. He makes no reference to the reading process or to any aspect of the child's perceptual development. The fact that adults find all the typefaces in common use equally legible (as measured by 'rate of work') may be irrelevant, rather than basic, to the requirements of a young child learning to read. In contrast to Tinker, Vernon (1971) takes into account results of studies carried out in many related fields of research, e.g., studies concerning a child's ability to discriminate between letter and word forms and studies concerned with the nature of the reading process (i.e. the cognitive, linguistic, perceptual and motivational factors involved in learning how to read).

The work of Poulton (1965) may be quoted as an example of a detailed study on the legibility of different typefaces. He found that the Gill Medium typeface (the letters of which were judged by typographical experts to be fairly strongly differentiated) was read more easily (as measured by rate of reading and comprehension scores) than Grotesque 215 and two versions of Univers (less well differentiated typefaces). No differences (of statistical significance) were found between the legibility of the Gill Medium (sans serif) typeface and three examples of typefaces with serifs, the features of which were not as well differentiated as the Gill Medium. Contrary to the findings of Burt, Poulton found no differences in legibility between all the serif and sans serif typefaces tested. A difference (though not significant statistically) in legibility between old face, transitional and modern was found. It was a complete reversal of the results reported by Burt who found old face the most legible and modern the least.

Poulton's study seems to indicate that neither serifs (as suggested by Burt) nor highly differentiated letter forms necessarily increase legibility. The importance of isolated distinctive features was investigated by Neisser (1963). He considered that legibility depended on the *'totality of features'* which made up the whole form of a letter or word. These features were thought as being 'simultaneously and multiply' processed in the perception of total form. The conclusions reached by Neisser appear to be compatible with Burt's approach to the legibility of different typefaces.

Research into the perceptual processes which determine the way in which we read print under normal reading conditions has produced results that are relevant to typography. We have already noted in a previous chapter that the fluent reader processes only part of what he sees. The more fluent he becomes, the less use he makes of graphic symbols to obtain meaning from the text. The question that must be asked is whether this progress to fluency involves the development of any systematic scanning procedure which enables the reader to avoid detailed inspection of the printed text. As long ago as 1908, Huey drew attention to the finding that the practised reader relied on the upper coastline of print for information. Kolers (in Gilliland, 1972) demonstrated that for a person reading systematically from left to right, the right hand side of letters is more informative. Kolers also found that typefaces which emphasized bold down strokes, impeded smooth visual

Figure 12: *Comparative legibility of upper and lower coastlines of print*

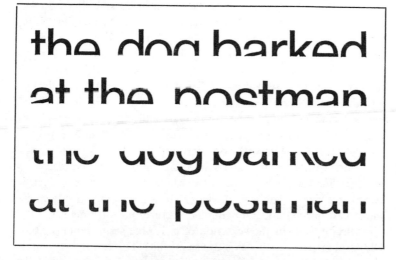

processing. He considered this to be supporting evidence to show that the skilled reader used the right hand side of the letter more than the left.

These experimental findings would seem to suggest that we could improve the legibility of a typeface by:

i. emphasizing distinguishing characteristics that appear on the top coastline of a word;

ii. arranging distinguishing clues to a letter's recognition, on the right hand side of the letter.

However, the research literature has also demonstrated that legibility is far too complex a concept for us to be able to improve it merely by simple manipulations such as these. The process of extracting meaning from print—for the skilled reader, at least—is one in which perception interacts with interpretation, anticipation and consolidation of thought. Peripheral sensory input enters a complex cerebral network, and it would be naive to expect that simple variations in the input could be measured by exact concomitant variations in the whole process. Nevertheless it should be possible to identify some basic points as guidelines in achieving maximum legibility. Prince (1967) suggests that a print scientifically devised to meet high standards of visual acuity may not be the one best suited to meet the needs of the reader. He attributes this to the establishment of preference patterns early in life. Prince recommends a conventional style of typeface, not because it satisfies high standards of visual acuity but because it 'matches up' with word images already in the brain. He suggests 'that a *Spartan type* would be better for all people if they could start and continue through life with this best form of type, but unless it is used universally, its advantages are hardly worth considering'.

Burt concludes his discussion on legibility of typefaces by saying: 'For the very young there would be a great advantage in selecting a single legible set of letter-shapes, keeping strictly to the lower case forms, and allowing no picturesque divergences.' The difficulty remains in the selection of a 'legible set of letter-shapes'. Old face, modern, with serifs or sans serifs? The research literature has not answered the question. What it has done is point to a 'totality of features' which together, or in various combinations, can increase the legibility of a typeface.

The interrelationship of size of type, leading, length of line and weight of print

The size of type, the spacing between the lines (leading), the length of line and the weight of print are interrelated factors that affect the legibility of a particular typeface. Decisions affecting the size of any one of these factors cannot be considered in isolation from the others. Thus a printer who wished to increase the size of typeface in a book from 12 points to 14 points, would need to consider altering the leading to increase the spacing between the lines, to lengthen the line of print to include the same number of words in the line and possibly to increase the weight of the typeface to maintain standards of visual acuity. In this way the standards of legibility operating for the 12 point typeface would be maintained (or possibly improved upon).

Research studies in this area of typographical research have been

Sammy loved to be busy. He was never happier than when he was chuff-chuffing out of Derry Station on another trip to Uptown.

Three miles out of Derry the track climbed a steep hill, but Sammy knew how to take this part of the journey. 'Steady-and-slow!' he would say to himself as he went puff-puffing up the hill.

When he reached the top he would give a toot on his whistle, and go rushing down the other side, pretending that he was the Flying Scotsman. He loved to hear the clickety-click, clickety-click of the coaches hurrying along behind him.

Exactly on time he would pull into Uptown Station and come to a stop with a screech of brakes and a hiss of steam. The passengers all loved Sammy and often they would give him a friendly nod as they hurried past him towards the ticket-collector.

'Good old Sam,' they would say. 'Always on time is our Sammy.'

But now Sammy was feeling very sad. One Saturday morning the Station-master had come to visit him in his engine-shed. He began by praising Sammy, telling him how well he had done his work. He called Sammy 'a faithful servant'. And Sammy smiled rather sadly for he knew that the Station-master was bringing bad news.

The Station-master looked down at his boots. Then he said, 'Sammy, I have sad news for you. On Monday Danny the Diesel is coming to take over your run.'

of limited practical value. A scientist when designing his experiment, observes the law of the single variable, i.e. he allows one factor to change while holding all others constant. This is good experimental technique, but if applied to this area of research the number of specimens required to replicate the necessary changes in combinations of factors is too unwieldy. The cost of printing the specimens would be considered prohibitive by most researchers. The outcome of this situation has been the development of an experimental design which has limited the necessary replications and combinations of different factors. Normally one variable only is measured, e.g. length of line. The conclusions reached in such experiments have little relevance to the normal situation as found in the printing of books. The complexity of the problem can be illustrated by a quotation taken from Buckingham's *New Data on Typography of Textbooks* (1931). Unfortunately, the situation as viewed by Buckingham has altered little over the past 43 years.

'In one especially good investigation a piece of printed matter is set in 10 point type on an 80 mm line—a perfectly proper and normal arrangement. Both shorter and longer lines, all set in 10 point type, are compared one by one with the 80 mm line and each time the 80 mm line is read more easily. From this, of course, one can conclude nothing as to the universal superiority of an 80 mm line. One cannot even say (although the investigators in this case suggest it) that a line of 80 mm is best for 10 point type. The results are valid only for the interlinear spacing employed, and the investigators do not tell us what that is. Widen the spacing and the probability is that a longer line may be employed to advantage. In fact, the situation is more complicated; the results are valid only for the series of type used with its characteristic shape of the letters, its height of the typeface on the body (all 10 point is not the same height), its expansion or right-and-left spreadoutness, and its width of heavy and light strokes. Accordingly, the printer, not knowing what series of type he may use, nor the spacing he may have between the lines, must be very sanguine if he supposes that merely by setting 10 point type on an 80 mm line he is attaining desirable results. As a matter of fact, he

Three miles out of Derry the track climbed a steep hill, but Sammy knew how to take this part of the journey. 'Steady-and-slow!' he would say to himself as he went puff-puffing up the hill.

When he reached the top he would give a toot on his whistle, and go rushing down the other side, pretending that he was the Flying Scotsman. He loved to hear the clickety-click, clickety-click of the coaches hurrying along behind him.

Exactly on time he would pull into Uptown Station and come to a stop with a screech of brakes and a hiss of steam. The passengers all loved Sammy and often they would give him a friendly nod as they hurried past him towards the ticket-collector.

'Good old Sam,' they would say. 'Always on time is our Sammy.'

But now Sammy was feeling very sad. One Saturday morning the Station-master had come to visit him in his engine-shed. He began by praising Sammy, telling him how well he had done his work. He called Sammy 'a faithful servant'. And Sammy smiled rather sadly for he knew that the Station-master was bringing bad news.

The Station-master looked down at his boots. Then he said, 'Sammy, I have sad news for you. On Monday Danny the Diesel is coming to take over your run.'

supposes no such thing. He realises the essentials are missing and probably wonders how the investigators "got that way".'

The article published by Buckingham in 1931 should be referred to, both as a *comprehensive review of past literature* published in this field of research and as an example of *an experimental design* which has succeeded in investigating the relationship between three interchanging factors. His experiment gives a great insight into the nature of the problem by indicating:

i. the great quantity and cost of experimental material required in running an experiment of this type;

ii. the importance of the content of the material and the relationship this has to the format of type in which it is printed;

iii. the expectations of the children in the experiment and how these vary according to social background, past experience, etc.

Buckingham used a modern typeface in the experiment (Monotype No. 8). Great efforts were made to find three stories suitable for grade two children which would have high interest value and not be difficult to read. The three stories were each printed in 18 different ways. Three sizes of type were used; 18 point, 14 point and 12 point. For each type size there were three line lengths; 24 picas (four inches), 21 picas ($3\frac{1}{2}$ inches) and $14\frac{1}{2}$ picas ($2\frac{5}{12}$ inches), each with either two or three amounts of leading; five point, four point and three point. A total of 2,010 seven-year-old children were tested. Both speed and comprehension measures of legibility were used. (This consisted of timing the reading test and then giving a comprehension test.)

Buckingham found that a 12 point type with a $14\frac{1}{2}$ pica line length and three point leading was read more rapidly than any other specimen. As far as speed was concerned the 12 point type could be set in a materially longer line (e.g. 21 picas) without any loss in legibility, *provided leading was increased to 4 points*. (This is of course relevant only to print set in the modern typeface Monotype No. 8.) If the size of type is increased to 14 point and the line is kept short, the leading may be reduced to three points with legibility still remaining high. Short lines in most combinations were more easily read. The speed rankings given by Buckingham for the first eight combinations of type are shown in Table 1.

TABLE 1: *Speed rankings for combinations of type*

RANK ORDER FOR SPEED	SIZE OF TYPE (POINTS)	LENGTH OF LINE (PICAS)	LEADING (POINTS)
1	12	14½	3
2	12	21	4
3	14	14½	3
4	12	14½	4
5	18	21	4
6	18	21	3
7	14	21	3
8	14	24	3

The order of rankings obtained for comprehension scores were very different from those obtained for speed reading, e.g. an 18 point type, set in a 24 pica line length with three point leading, was ranked 14th in speed scores but was second in comprehension scores. Eighteen point, 21 picas and five point leading was the worst combination in speed scores but better than average in comprehension. However, the trend for the combinations which were low in speed ranking to improve greatly their ranking in comprehension scores was not consistent, though there was some evidence of reversal.

For length of line, comprehension scores did not show the clear trend that was evident with speed scores. Buckingham doubts whether comprehension scores are valid measures of legibility and postulates that their merit may be limited to acting as a control on speed (i.e. ensuring a degree of understanding of the text).

For children of this age (seven years) Buckingham favours the use of a 12 point typeface (for Monotype No. 8) which, on combined speed and comprehension scores, fared better than any combination of 18 point type. He makes the reservation that specimens which rank at the very top of speed and comprehension scores, may be undesirable on other grounds (e.g. visual acuity).

The rankings of total page area for each specimen as calculated by Buckingham are listed in Table 2. These findings have significance as regards the cost of print (where cost equals the number of words to the square inch) in that the size of type and interlinear space may to some extent be substituted for one another. Thus, for example, when 14 point type is reduced to 12 point and at the same time given an added point of leading, the rankings for both cost and legibility are improved. Consideration should be given to Buckingham's findings in those cases where the opportunities for increasing the legibility of a text are restricted by such factors as size of page, the position, colour and size of illustrations and the cost of production.

TABLE 2: *Area and legibility compared for 18 specimens, in a book of 20,000 words (Buckingham)*

Size of Type (Points)	SPECIMEN Length of Line (Picas)	Leading (Points)	NO. OF FULL PAGES	RANK IN SPEED AND COMPREHENSION SCORES	TOTAL TYPE AREA Sq. in.	Rank
12	14½	3	108	3	1580	1
12	24	3	66	15	1584	2
12	21	3	76	12	1596	3
12	24	4	70	11	1680	4·5
12	21	4	80	2	1680	4·5
12	14½	4	116	1	1696	6
14	21	3	98	4	2058	7
14	24	3	86	13	2064	8
14	14½	3	142	6	2076	9
14	21	4	104	8	2184	10
14	14½	4	150	14	2194	11
14	24	4	92	9	2208	12
18	21	3	154	10	3234	13
18	24	3	138	7	3312	14
18	24	4	144	16	3456	15
18	21	4	166	5	3486	16
18	21	5	172	18	3612	17
18	24	5	152	7	3648	18

Buckingham's results have been described in some detail above because his research is one of the relatively few examples of a systematic experimental design applied to a substantial sample of children at an early stage in learning to read. Unlike Buckingham, the great majority of researchers in this field have not been concerned with measuring the relationship between different factors which interact to affect the legibility of a particular typeface. Instead studies have tended to isolate one factor (e.g. length of line) and measure it under different conditions, holding all other variables constant. That is, for all variations in the length of line, the typeface, the size of type, leading and weight of print are held constant. In these studies, the criteria against which legibility is measured include:

   i. the measurement of eye movements;
   ii. visibility measures;
   iii. speed of reading measures;
   iv. readers' opinions.

The nature of eye movements and their methods of measurement have been described in Section 1. Javal was the first to study eye movement patterns and relate them to suitable measures of line length, type size and leading (Huey 1908). He found that leading did not increase legibility appreciably and thought the interlinear space would be better used to increase the size of type. He also favoured the use of short lines, placing the maximum at 90 mm. He found that long lines of print caused eye strain and, unless the reader was prepared to move his head from side to side as he read, the degree of eye strain would increase with increases in the length of line. He attributed the eye strain to asymmetrical accommodation which occurred when fixation points were closer to one eye than to the other. Tinker (1965) measured the eye movement patterns of college students and found an increase in the number of fixations when reading a longer line of 43 picas (compared to 19 picas which Tinker regarded as an optimum line length). He also found a large increase (57 per cent) in the number of regressions made by the readers and a difficulty in making the return sweep to the beginning of the next line. The specimens for Tinker's experiment were printed in 10 point Scotch Roman lower case typeface set solid, that is with no leading. In a second experiment an 'excessively short line' (9 picas as compared to the standard of 19 picas) was found to present as many difficulties to the reader as did the longer line of 43 picas. The inefficiency of this length of line was attributed to the reader's difficulty in making full use of peripheral vision in the horizontal direction. Burt would suggest that the short length of line would interrupt the 'rhythm of reading'.

Prince (1967) in an article on print for the visually handicapped, recommends the adoption by printers of a standardized line length, preferably one of 36 picas, but one not less than 30 picas. He maintains that the short line, double-column style used by printers, is exceedingly inefficient, since it demands more eye excursions so that it takes longer to read a given amount of material; produces more hyphenations; and in some instances demands more paper. Prince also summarizes the reasons given for not exceeding an 18 point type for both normal and visually handicapped readers: first, the larger a type, the fewer words to a line unless the length of line is extended far beyond what is considered satisfactory. Secondly, when there are fewer words on a line, the number of excursions from the end of one line, to the beginning of the next is vastly increased, as are the number of hyphenations. Both these factors slow a reader and reduce his efficiency. Although there is no problem of *letter legibility*, there does arise a problem of *word legibility* when the direct span of vision cannot focus on the entire word. Carmichael and Dearborn (1972) tabulate the approximate number of letters which may be seen in a single horizontal line, for different sizes of type. For example, at a reading distance of 14 inches, six point type brings six letters within the foveal area (visual angle of 70 minutes), and 66 letters within a 12 degree field of vision; 12 point type brings only 3·5 letters within the foveal area, and 38 letters within the wider field of vision. Of course, the eye does not always 'see' all that the visual angle encompasses.

Luckiesh and Moss (1940) use eye blinking as a criterion against which to measure legibility of different typefaces, sizes of type, leading and weight of print. In the article 'Criteria of Readability' they have compared rate of blinking to speed of reading and found a marked discrepancy between these two measures of legibility. This disagreement between the two criteria was suggested by Buckingham in his recommendations for a 12 point typeface for seven-year-old readers based on speed of reading scores.

Luckiesh and Moss consider the optimum degree of boldness for a typeface to be related to four variables; size, the visibility of the individual printed characters, the *effective* amount of leading and the distracting influence of characters adjacent to those included in the perceptual span of the moment. Prince maintains that, for maximum legibility of letters, the image in the eye should consist of strokes which are never closer together than their own thickness. For a normal subject, the most legible dimensions of letters are those in which the width of letter is 80 per cent of its height, and the thickness of each stroke is not more than 20 per cent of its width. These dimensions have been calculated from visibility scores measured in the laboratory. Prince adds that once letters are formed into words, visibility criteria become less important as the familiarity of the word influences legibility. In *unfamiliar words*, Prince supports Luckiesh and Moss in saying that the positions of the various letters and their proximity to certain other letters influence their legibility.

Javal, Cohn, Weber, Griffing and Franz were amongst the first investigators who made specific recommendations as regards the legibility of typography for adult readers (Huey 1908, Spencer 1969). These recommendations were based primarily on the observation and detailed measurement of eye movement patterns. Where the technical methods of measurement were of a high standard, the results have provided an accurate and objective measure of the perceptual processes involved in reading print. It is argued by Luckiesh and Moss that quantitative measures such as eye blink, number of fixation pauses, number of regressions, etc., are the only valid criteria against which to measure the legibility of print. Speed of reading is regarded as an 'insensitive indicator of readability'. The authors attribute the insensitivity of this measure of legibility to the reader's tendency to '*compensate*' whenever the print he is reading becomes less legible. Carmichael and Dearborn (1972) quote Luckiesh and Moss as saying 'eyes may perform as well under poor conditions as under good—visual mechanisms will temporarily compensate for poor conditions of seeing by an increased expenditure of energy'. Carmichael and Dearborn do not oppose Luckiesh and Moss's theory, but point out the difficulty of evaluating it by quantitative measures. (They did, however, make extensive studies to discover whether visual fatigue could be used as a measure of legibility, but found with prolonged reading, no significant changes occurred.)

Speed of reading and readers' preferences have also been used as criteria of legibility. Both measures have the advantage of being easily applied to the normal reading situation. However, they possess the major disadvantage of being affected by the content of the material read. The reader's response to the material is influenced by his past experience and his expectations of the experimental situation. Hovde (1930) found context to be a more important factor in determining legibility than the physical characteristics of the type setting when reading rate was used as a criterion. Both Hovde and Tinker (1963) found readers based their preferences on the physical characteristics of the type, e.g. boldness of print, size of type, interlinear spacing, etc. Little agreement was found to exist between a reader's preference for a particular type and his performance as measured by reading speed. Zachrisson (1965) investigated the relationship between the preference expressed by children (grades 1–4) for a particular size of type and legibility (as measured by objective standards). He found a very low correlation between opinion and legibility and concluded by saying: 'Habit, experience, and the subjective ease of perceiving the text are one thing; performance seems to be another'. Thus the idiosyncratic nature of personal preferences may be a serious obstacle to precise experimentation in the study of legibility.

In conclusion it may be argued that no criterion, in isolation, can provide a suitable measure of legibility. The scientific accuracy of oculomotor patterns and visibility measurements provide useful insights into the perceptual and visual mechanisms involved in reading print. They may not provide an accurate measure of the processes involved in the normal reading situation. Speed of reading can be measured experimentally in conditions which provide a more accurate representation of the normal reading situation but may produce results which are confounded by factors operating outside the experimenter's control. Attempts have been made to limit the influence of these factors by control of the content of material, of the social background of subjects, or of their preferences. The point of difficulty is that the greater and more restrictive the controls, the less likely the experimental design will be representative of the normal reading situation.

Since the research literature offers few guidelines on the most suitable combination of typographic factors, it may be more appropriate to base decisions for young children's books on:
  i. The level of perceptual development of young children.
  ii. The nature of the reading process.

For example, by making lines of print the length of the phrase or sentence in books for very young children, the printer will help the child obtain meaning from the printed text. Carmichael and Dearborn (1972) recommend that a regular length of line should be introduced as early as possible to encourage the development of regular eye movement patterns. (Burt describes this as 'rhythm of reading'.) A type size should be large enough to enable ease of letter discrimination, but small enough to encourage word recognition rather than letter recognition. This would preclude the use of a type size larger than 18 points. Generous leading would appear appropriate for children in the early grades where perception and spatial difficulties are commonly found.

Recommendations for standards of legibility in children's books

A brief summary of six major studies carried out this century is included in this review to illustrate the methods used by investigators in the past, and to note their recommendations to printers for standards of legibility in children's books. Buckingham (1930) describes such findings as follows: 'Several of those who have given out standards have simply used their imagination; those who have made real investigations have obtained results of limited practical value.' Without questioning the validity of Buckingham's opinion we are able, by comparison of the various recommendations, to gain some insight into the nature of the research literature.

1. Shaw 1902

One of the first investigations into standards of legibility was reported more than 70 years ago by Shaw in 1902. He based his recommendations for type in children's textbooks on the results published by Cohn (a German investigator who worked with adult subjects). Shaw 'adjusts' Cohn's results by increasing the size of type. However the sizes recommended are of little value to the printers as the measurements given do not coincide with standard type sizes, e.g. 2·6 mm, the size recommended for grade 1 falls between 18 point and 14 point; and 2·0 mm, the size recommended for grade 2 falls between 14 point and 12 point. Shaw confuses the term 'leading' with interlinear spacing. (Even if lines are 'set solid' some space exists between the letters.) The 4·5 leading recommended for grade 1 would mean something like 15 points which is not plausible.

TABLE 3: *Type dimensions recommended by Shaw in 'School Hygiene' 1902*

GRADE	MINIMUM X-HEIGHT OF TYPE (MM.)	LEADING (MM.)
1	2·6	4·5
2	2·0	4·0
3	2·0	4·0
4	1·8	3·6
Above 4	1·6	3·0

Huey (1908) based his conclusions on the work of several investigators, especially Cohn, Weber and Javal. He quotes Shaw's recommendations in *School Hygiene* as 'the most usable approximate statement of what may be insisted on, for the sake of uniformity' and he adds that some of the leading recommended by Shaw may be sacrificed for a larger type.

2. British Association for the Advancement of Science 1913

In 1913 the British Association for the Advancement of Science published a 'Standard Typographical Table'. The Association recommended an 18 point type size for seven–eight years (as 14 point is below the minimum of 2·5 mm recommended). This is considerably larger than the print normally found in books for children of this age. The amount of leading (4·0 mm) is small in comparison to what would be expected with an 18 point type size.

TABLE 4: '*Standard Typographical Table*' 1913

AGE OF READER	MIN. HEIGHT FACE OF SHORT LETTERS (MM.)	MIN. INTERLINEAR SPACE (MM.)	MAX. LENGTH OF LINE (MM.)
Under 7 years	3·5	6·5	—
7–8 years	2·5	4·0	100
8–9 years	2·0	2·9	93
9–12 years	1·8	2·4	93
Over 12 years	1·58	2·2	93

3. Kerr 1926

Kerr (1926) suggested smaller sizes than those reported by the British Association. He based his recommendations on figures published by the American School Hygiene Association (1911) and his own experimental inquiry. The minimal type sizes recommended to the printer by Kerr are listed in Table 5.

TABLE 5: *Minimal type sizes 1926*

Infants under 7 years	— 24 point
7–9 years	— 14 point
over 9 years	— 14 point

The interspace between lines not less than $\frac{1}{35}$ of the length of the line (to aid in picking up the next line in its sweep backwards).

4. Blackhurst 1927

Blackhurst (1927) who carried out extensive experimentation in size of type, leading and length of line with children in the first four grades of school, was in agreement with the recommendations made by Shaw and Huey. His experimental results were based on speed of reading measures. In grade 1, changes in type size were said to have no appreciable affect on reading. (Sizes ranging from 14 point to 30 point showed no differences in scores.) A similar result was found in grade 2. (The range in type size was 10 point to 24 point.) In grades 3 and 4, 18 point was found to give the highest scores. The amount of leading was said to have no significant effect on speed of reading in the first four grades.

5. Burt 1959

Burt (1959) preferred to formulate standards in terms of optimum sizes. He adds that words, for the very young (below nine years) should be well spaced with an em-space as a minimum instead of an en-space as a maximum.

TABLE 6: *Typographical standards for children's reading books, recommended by Burt 1959*

AGE	TYPEFACE (POINTS)	NO. OF LETTERS IN A LINE OF 4"	LENGTH OF LINE (IN.)	INTERLINEAR SPACE (IN.)
Under 7	24	30	5	0·26
7–8	18	38	4	0·17
8–9	16	45	3·5	0·16
9–10	14	52	3·75	0·13
10–12	12	58	4	0·12
Over 12	11	60	4·5	0·10

6. Tinker 1959

Tinker (1959), on the basis of research evidence and publishing experience, suggests that type size for grade 1 should be 14 point to 18 point and for grades 2 and 3, 12 point to 14 point. For the upper grades (4 to 8) 10, 11 or 12 point should be used. These type sizes are smaller than those recommended previously, although they follow closely the results reached by Buckingham in 1931. Tinker found large disagreement in the research literature concerning length of line and space between the lines. Some studies reported failure to detect any association between reading speed and line length or leading. Others produced recommendations of a very specific nature: for example, Blackhurst recommended a 24 pica (four-inch) line for use in all primary grades. Tinker summarized the available evidence and found that line length may vary from 16 to 30 picas in the primary grades without any loss in reading speed. No pattern emerged from the research literature as regards the quantity of leading to be recommended. Tinker suggests that a 'satisfactory agreement' might well be four to six point leading in grade 1, three to four point in grade 2 and two or three point in grades 3 and 4. Above the 4th grade leading should be the same as for adult readers, i.e. two point leading with type size 10, 11 or 12 point.

TABLE 6: *Recommendations made by Tinker for type in children's books 1959*

GRADE	SIZE OF TYPE (POINTS)	LENGTH OF LINE (PICAS)	LEADING (POINTS)
1	14–18	16–22	4–6
2–3	12–14	18–24	3–4
Over 4	10, 11 or 12	18–24	2

Margins

Burt in *A Psychological Study of Typography* states:

'There can be little doubt that books with excessively narrow margins are more apt to produce visual fatigue . . . moreover, when the type area extends nearly to the edge of the paper, the eye of the younger reader is apt to swing right off the page. With adults the effect of the broader margin would seem to be chiefly aesthetic.'

The conventional margins used in books reduce the printed area to approximately half of the total page size and are in a ratio of 1 (inner margin) to $1\frac{1}{2}$ (head) to 2 (outside edge) to $2\frac{1}{2}$ (foot) or $1\frac{1}{2} : 2 : 3 : 4$ (Spencer 1969 p. 46). Many book designers consider margins of these dimensions desirable on aesthetic grounds. The unit of a book is not regarded as a single page but a double-spread and the optical centre of a page is higher than the true centre. (Tinker, 1965, reports that readers overestimate the area of print on a page by approximately 25 per cent.)

Writing in 1881, Weber (one of the earliest authorities on legibility) stated that margins were not necessary. This viewpoint has been strongly criticized by Burt and others (Cohn, Dearborn) who argue that books with excessively narrow margins produce visual fatigue. Burt (1959) claims that margins keep out peripheral colour stimuli and prevent the eye (in the backward movement) from swinging off the page. Unfortunately he gives no evidence to support these conclusions.

On the other hand Paterson and Tinker (reported in *Bases for Effective Reading* 1965, p. 183) found no significant differences in results of speed reading between material printed with margins (left and right) $\frac{7}{8}$ inch wide and material printed 'without margins'. (Spencer, 1969, p. 45, reports that margins of $\frac{1}{16}$ inch were in fact used by Paterson and Tinker in this experiment.) These tests were carried out with adults and consequently the results may have little relevance to the reading situation as encountered by young children.

Due to the lack of significant differences in speed of reading scores, Tinker maintains that margins cannot be justified in terms of legibility, but rather in terms of their aesthetic appeal. Spencer (1969) criticizes the short duration of the test period used by Paterson and Tinker ($1\frac{3}{4}$ minutes) and suggests that a longer period may yield a different result. Tinker also overlooks the practical advantages of margins. The inner margin should be wide enough to prevent the curvature of the paper from obscuring the end of the printed line. Margins also provide a place for the finger to hold the page without obscuring the text.

In the absence of research evidence, more appropriate guidelines for the use of margins in children's books, may be gained from a study of:

ii. the practical considerations of a young child reading a book;
ii. the immaturity of perceptual development where an absence of margins may well distract the young reader from the text.

Justified versus unjustified composition

If the reader examines any text book in front of him he is almost certain to find the spaces between the words vary in size, and that by varying the spacing, and by sometimes using hyphenation, the printer has achieved a straight right-hand margin. This is known as justified composition. Where regular spacing between words is maintained (such as in typescript) the lines of print will have an uneven length, giving the right-hand margin a ragged appearance. This is unjustified composition. In addition to regular spacing, unjustified setting contains fewer, if any, hyphenations. This is an important consideration when lines of print are short and the type size is large, as found in the printing of young children's books.

The relative advantages of one form of composition over another, which are related specifically to layout and cost factors, are straightforward and well known to publishers. The controversy that exists over justification concerns the relative legibility, instructional value and aesthetic appeal of the two methods of composition. Writing in 1904, T. L. De Vinne (Zachrisson 1965) criticized unjustified setting as being aesthetically unacceptable, although arresting to the eye. The consideration of aesthetic acceptability versus the impact nature of unjustified setting became a subject of detailed investigation. Research studies have since dismissed the findings of De Vinne on the grounds that most subjects *fail to notice* the difference in appearance between the two compositions. Aesthetic appeal was found to be related more to the context of the material or to other typographical factors such as typeface, size of print, use of headings, etc., than to any consideration of inter-word spacing, hyphenation or raggedness of the right-hand margin. It is possible that justified or unjustified margins may have some influence on legibility, even though the difference is not perceived consciously. Research studies have therefore tried to measure any differences in legibility or instructional value (i.e. the ability to aid learning) that may exist between justified and unjustified composition.

The criteria commonly used to measure legibility (Zachrisson, 1965; Fabrizio *et al.*, 1967; and Hartley *et al.*, 1973) are the

to think they do. Hartley and Mills base this reservation on the recent studies made into the reading process (Smith 1971), whereby fluent readers make very little use of graphic symbols to gain meaning from the text. On the basis of evidence from the study of eye movements in reading, Hartley and Mills suggest that the difference between a fast and slow reader is not the speed it takes his eyes to move along a line of print, but the nature of the information he perceives with each fixation (Kolers, 1969). In addition a point must be taken from Smith (1971) who suggests that information contributed from the brain is as important to reading as information contributed from the eye.

These reservations suggest that differences between justified and unjustified composition cannot be measured using fluent readers and easy texts, as the small variations in typographical design will not be noticed under these conditions.

Numerals
Ranging (or lining) numerals are of uniform height, and found in modern faces of print. They can be compared to the hanging numerals found in old faces which have ascenders and descenders above and below the line of print. Burt in *A Psychological Study of Typography* (p. 9) notes that teachers claim the ranging numerals of

Figure 15: *Ranging and hanging numerals*

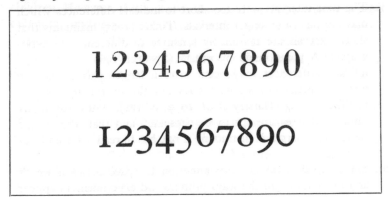

1234567890

1234567890

modern faces to be more easily read by children (especially the Scotch Roman and Times Roman) than the ascending and descending numerals of the older faces which cause 'appreciable hesitation', particularly when the figures are grouped.

Tinker (1965) states that a study of the legibility of numerals requires consideration of several related problems. They include: 'the relative legibility of digits; modern versus old style digits; reading of numbers grouped in mathematical tables; numbers and other symbols in formulae and Roman versus arabic numerals.' It is not the purpose of this section to discuss each of these considerations as a separate issue in the legibility of numerals. A concise summary of the major recommendations, going as far back as 1827 with recommendations by Babbage, is given by Tinker. Reference should be made to this chapter for precise details. Results from Tinker's own studies indicate that old face (or hanging) numerals with ascenders and descenders are easier to perceive in isolation than modern (or ranging) numerals. This difference in legibility was found using perceptibility measures of distance and short exposure, and consequently refers to the individual letter's visual acuity at a distance. Tinker found no differences between the two styles in the speed and accuracy with which they were read in groups. He concludes by saying 'in a normal reading situation, differences in legibility between the two typefaces are unimportant'.

Soar (1955) tested the hypothesis that with increases in either height or width of a number, the increase in visual acuity may be attributed to the alteration in the *proportions* of the number rather than to the increase in area. Using a tachistoscopic device which controlled exposure and illumination of the number, Soar found (by holding area constant) that the most visible combinations were: height to width 10 : 7·5 and stroke width to height 1 : 10. Berger (1948) found that the visibility of numbers improved as their width was increased. The difficulty arises that many of the studies on numbers (such as those by Soar and Berger) are more concerned with measures of visual acuity rather than with the wider concept of legibility. It has been stated in previous sections of this review, that optimal levels of visual acuity are not always a guide to what the reader regards as the most legible or most suitable form of type. This applies to numbers in the same way it applies to letters or the use of colour and illustrations. Burt (1959) states that the question of legibility between the two types of numerals has been greatly oversimplified and that the effect of *habit* has been overlooked in studies concerning legibility of numerals.[1]

A study carried out by Flores (1960) entitled 'Methods of comparing the legibility of printed numerals', gives credence to the point made by Burt. Flores found, under conditions of marginal illumination and observation (as measured by a tachistoscope), that the ability to distinguish between the numbers of five different founts, depended mainly on the individual numbers being critically different from each other. These differences were related to the variations in the pattern of the number. A second experiment providing limited judgment time, but adequate conditions for preparation, found that identification of numbers depended to a great extent on the similarity of the type to that dealt with in daily experience and consequently upon the amount of learning present. Flores concluded by suggesting that where a situation calls for numbers to be identified with a minimum of learning but under favourable presentation conditions (such as when a child is learning to read) a fount with close resemblance to familiar arabic numerals is recommended. When immediate identification of numbers under marginal light and examination circumstances is required (such as for use on a dial face on the instrument panel of a car) it would appear that a fount with highly differentiated patterns would be superior (e.g. air force fount).

Extensive research into the legibility of numerals has been carried out in recent years. It has been of a very specific nature and concerns mainly the use of numerals in visual displays (e.g. instrument panels, bill boards, road signs), mathematical tables and

---

[1]Burt emphasizes the difficulty of making general statements concerning the relative legibility of hanging and ranging numerals. He points out that the 3 and 5 of Plantin and Imprint are easily confused. On the other hand, with ranging figures, 3 and 8 are often confused, especially in reading small mathematical tables.

Figure 16: *Founts of numerals for use on dials, computer displays and public transport*

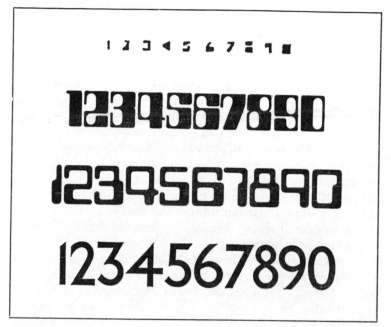

electronically operated equipment. Two books which will provide an introduction to the research literature in this field are Spencer (1969) *The Visible Word* and Foster (1972) *Legibility Research Abstracts*.

Other considerations

In addition to the legibility of the typographical factors already mentioned, there exist many special printing situations that require detailed consideration. A selection has been made based on the criterion of relevance to the printing of *children's* books. A brief review only of the research literature is given for each consideration.

(a) *Punctuation*

Opinions as to the use of punctuation marks in children's books range from: 'Punctuation marks are ignored completely by children and need to be pointed out to them'; to: 'Punctuation marks cause great confusion to the young child learning to read and should consequently be used as sparingly as possible.'

Prince (1967) in a study with normal and visually handicapped adults, found that the full stop and comma needed to be enlarged beyond the sizes in current use. This he stressed 'is not just reflected in the data and observations in scientific tests, but is voluntarily and persistently commented upon by a large number of both normal and subnormal vision subjects used in reading tests' (p. 38). Prince recommends that the full stop be increased to 30 per cent of the height of the lower case letter 'o' and the comma to 55 per cent of this height. He also recommends (on the basis of his research with the visually handicapped) that the hyphenation should be avoided owing to its poor legibility.

Spencer (1969) takes note of the study carried out by Ovink who found that while the shape of the dot on the lower case 'i' and 'j' was irrelevant, a big, heavy dot greatly contributed to legibility. It may therefore be necessary to increase the size of punctuation marks to draw the attention of the young reader. Confusion should not occur if punctuation marks have distinct forms and are introduced into the text at an appropriate level of reading efficiency.

(b) *Form of type used for emphasis*

When printing children's books it is often necessary to emphasize or draw attention to a particular word or group of words, such as a heading or a new letter or word. Conventional methods used to emphasize print are italics, bold face, capitals, change in colour or by underlining. There has been considerable research into the use of different forms of print, but relatively few studies have been carried out with children, except for those concerning colour as an aid to learning. (These studies are treated in the next section.)

If the printer introduces a change in type design, the print will stand out from the remainder of the text. The difficulty arises that the child may find the changes in the form of print distracting and rather than aiding learning it may in fact hinder. An example of this may be found in the Dale Readers (a phonic method of teaching reading popularized by Nellie Dale in 1899) where different colours are used to print individual sounds. The system may help the child to recognize individual sounds, but may also hinder him from the main task of learning to read by distracting his attention from the word form. A printer should therefore give careful consideration to his reasons for emphasizing a word. If the purpose of emphasis is to *act as a cue* to aid learning then consideration should be given to the respective legibility of italics, bold face, capitals, change in colour and underlining as alternative modes of emphasis.

Investigation into the legibility of roman lower case and italic typefaces by Paterson and Tinker in 1940 (reported in Tinker, 1965, p. 134), has shown that roman lower case is easier to read than italic print and is generally preferred by readers. No significant differences were found in speed of reading between bold face (that is, heavy black print) and ordinary lower case, although bold face was said to have greater visual acuity than ordinary print. Readers were found by Paterson and Tinker, to prefer material printed in ordinary lower case to material printed in bold face.

Luckiesh and Moss (1940) found that ordinary lower case and bold face were read more quickly than material printed in italics or capitals. Tinker (1965) supports the findings of Luckiesh and Moss. He suggests that the higher legibility of ordinary lower case and bold face over capitals and italics, is due to the *overall shape* of the roman lower case word form which provides an important cue to word recognition. (Research evidence would suggest that only parts of the letters of a word provide the essential cues for the word's identification: Kolers, 1969; Biemieller, 1970). Tinker also considers the reading of italic print to be more affected (than roman lower case) by marginal changes in other conditions (e.g. poorer quality paper or poor illumination), which tends to retard reading efficiency. Shaw (1969, p. 21) points out the poor visual acuity of italic print in comparison to roman lower case, mentioning the relative light weight, fussy design and tendency for italic print to appear smaller when mixed with roman lower case. On the other hand, it may be the reader's lack of familiarity with material printed all in italic or capital letters which contributes to the poorer performance in speed reading tests, compared to material printed in roman lower case.

Coloured letters have varied legibility and aesthetic appeal. Kerr in *Fundamentals of School Health* quotes Gibson (Cheshire Report, 1912) as saying that 'black letters are visible at 128 inches, blue and red at 100 and yellow at 48.' Perceptibility measures such as these may not be relevant to the printing of books where the reading distance is normally 14 inches. It is surprising that recommendations such as these where so many confounding factors are operant (e.g. variations in chroma, hue, illumination, background, etc.) have received such widespread acceptance. Tinker (1965) ranks various colour combinations from most legible to least legible on the basis of perceptibility measures and speed of reading. The rankings correlate highly with brightness contrast ratios (i.e. between print and paper) and reader preferences. The first four rankings were black print on white paper, blue on white, black on yellow and green on white. Vickerstaff *et al.* (1950), in an investigation into the visual acuity and legibility of colour combinations, reported similar findings.

Klare *et al.* (1955) found that the patterning of reading material (by underlining important points) improved adult comprehension of the text. Speed of reading was not decreased, to a significant extent, by underlining sections of the text. Subjects also found the material as aesthetically acceptable as unpatterned material. Klare *et al.* make the reservation that the less able reader may be hindered by such presentation unless he is told what it means. This may apply also to young children learning to read, where underlining may act as a distraction rather than a cue, thus hindering the child's comprehension of the text.

It is recommended that where emphasis is required to draw attention to a new word, and therefore where legibility is paramount, bold face (and possibly underlining) should be used. Capitals, italics and the use of colour all decrease legibility. However considerations of legibility may be sacrificed for purposes of impact, designed to gain the child's attention. The lower legibility may be compensated by increased attention which the child gives to the printed material.

(c) *Paper surface*

The nature of the paper surface involves a study of its thickness, opacity, texture and finish (that is, matt or gloss). Research studies have used three techniques to investigate the effect of paper surface on legibility: they are, visibility measures, speed of reading and perceptibility at a distance. Carmichael and Dearborn (1972) quote several studies which have used all three techniques and found no significant differences in measures of legibility between paper surfaces of varying qualities and textures. For example, Stanton and Burtt (1935) used a white glossy-coated paper as the standard. No significant differences were found between the standard and 'dull-coated', 'white-antique' and 'ivory-antique' surfaces. Paterson and Tinker (1940) compared egg-shell paper with white enamel, artisan-enamel and flint enamel paper. These four papers represent degrees of gloss from 22·9 per cent for egg-shell to 95·1 per cent for flint enamel. Again no significant differences were found. However Tinker and Paterson reported that there was a great variation in reader preference for the different types of paper, with 75 per cent (of 224 readers) preferring the egg-shell paper and only six per cent the flint enamel (see Tinker, 1965). Tinker concludes that most readers 'obviously dislike reading print on highly glossy paper'. On the other hand, Roethlein (1912), who used a distance method to investigate the legibility of letters in nine typefaces printed on two different types of paper (glazed and matt), found subjects expressed no preferences for either kind of paper used.

Luckiesh and Moss (1938) obtained visibility measurements for print on several kinds of paper surface which varied from dull to fairly glossy finish. Little variation in visibility was found. They concluded that such papers, which may vary considerably in surface character, do not materially affect the visibility of print if good black ink and type are used.

Tinker (1965) has made two reservations concerning the interpretation of experimental data. Firstly the effects of different paper surfaces on legibility have only been tested over short periods of time. It seems probable that long periods of reading print on glossy paper would contribute to eyestrain and fatigue. Secondly, experimental results are obtained under good lighting conditions, whereas the normal reading situation frequently takes place under poor conditions. The combination of badly diffused illumination and glossy paper will cause fatigue and eyestrain. Tinker is quoted as saying (p. 167):

'Even moderately glazed paper produces specular[1] glare when the illumination is not well diffused and when the page of reading material is held at such an angle that the reflected light shines directly into the reader's eyes. This is uncomfortable and vision is impaired.'

Tinker's account of the thickness of paper to be used for printing of books in *Bases for Effective Reading* (p. 168) is particularly relevant to this review. It is quoted in full:

'Thickness of paper used for printing must also be considered. Although no experimental data are available on the subject, there are sufficient reasons for employing paper of adequate thickness and opacity so that print on the back side does not show through. When print does show through, the resulting "shadows" blur the print on the front side. When the paper is lightweight or thin, these shadows become fairly prominent and reduce visibility of print. Quick discrimination of letters and words becomes difficult. While it may be more economical to print books and magazines on very thin paper, such practice is indefensible from the viewpoint of hygienic vision.'

The research studies named by Tinker (1965) and Carmichael and Dearborn (1972) have all been carried out with adult subjects. Their findings are relevant to the paper used for printing of children's books in that they suggest the *problems of visibility* that occur when paper is too transparent (allowing print from the

---

[1] Specular – as from a mirror.

reverse side to show through) or too glossy (resulting in high levels of reflected glare).

To be able to print natural looking pictures in children's books, some degree of compromise between a matt and a glossy enamel surface is deemed necessary. In books where the pictorial content far outweighs the printed words, it may be acceptable for a glossier surface to be used. The likelihood of visual fatigue or eyestrain occurring under these reading conditions is extremely slight. However, where the pictorial content is a minor consideration, the problems of visibility suggested in the adult studies should be taken into account by the printer, together with the cost of the paper and the size of the book (a dense paper making large books fatiguing to hold).

Sammy loved to be busy. He was never happier than when he was chuff-chuffing out of Derry Station on another trip to Uptown.

Three miles out of Derry the track climbed a steep hill, but Sammy knew how to take this part of the journey. 'Steady-and-slow!' he would say to himself as he went puff-puffing up the hill.

When he reached the top he would give a toot on his whistle, and go rushing down the other side, pretending that he was the Flying Scotsman. He loved to hear the clickety-click, clickety-click of the coaches hurrying along behind him.

Exactly on time he would pull into Uptown Station and come to a stop with a screech of brakes and a hiss of steam. The passengers all loved Sammy and often they would give him a friendly nod as they hurried past him towards the ticket-collector.

'Good old Sam,' they would say. 'Always on time is our Sammy.'

But now Sammy was feeling very sad. One Saturday morning the Station-master had come to visit him in his engine-shed. He began by praising Sammy, telling him how well he had done his work. He called Sammy 'a faithful servant'. And Sammy smiled rather sadly for he knew that the Station-master was bringing bad news.

The Station-master looked down at his boots. Then he said, 'Sammy, I have sad news for you. On Monday Danny the Diesel is coming to take over your run.'

And so on Saturday evening Sammy made his last trip to Derry, and on Monday he began to shunt the coaches and trucks in the station yard. He did not look up when Danny the Diesel drew out of Derry pulling the nine-five, Sammy's special run. He just kept his eyes on the track and let the steam sizzle sadly out of his chimney.

Day after day Sammy worked in the railway yard, pushing and shunting, but seldom getting a chance to go faster than three miles an hour—or maybe four.

His fine, shining, black paintwork soon became dirty and dull, so that even his friends, the Uptown passengers, sometimes did not recognise him.

Danny the Diesel was very popular. He could travel so fast and so smoothly. Because of this, more and more people began to travel on the Derry to Uptown line. Instead of four coaches Danny had to have five, then six, and sometimes seven. And there came a day when he was asked to pull eight coaches.

Sammy was just a little jealous when he saw Danny pulling smoothly out of Derry with eight fine new coaches packed with passengers.

The station yard was very quiet after Danny had gone. With a trickle of steam escaping from a little crack in his boiler Sammy dozed and later fell asleep. He was dreaming that he was racing the Flying Scotsman all the way to Edinburgh, when he awoke with a start. Someone was calling to him.

Colour and Illustration

A. The use of colour

THE USE OF colour in the printing of books has been investigated extensively and while some studies have provided clear guidelines as regards the legibility of different colours, others have served only to demonstrate the intricacies and difficulties that are involved in any measure of legibility.

Colour is used in the printing of books for aesthetic and motivational reasons. Children and adults find colour more attractive than black and white and consequently are more likely to choose a book printed in colour than one printed in black and white, although it is generally accepted that the content of the book acts as the prime motivational factor (D'Arcy, 1973).

Colour is also used as an aid to learning. The planned introduction of colour to black and white print or illustration is said to make the monochrome material more meaningful to the child thus increasing his retention or learning of the information. Gattegno (1962) and Jones (1968) have developed separate methods of teaching young children to read by using colour combinations to give additional phonetic information. A discussion of the theory underlying these approaches to the teaching of reading, is a separate issue which is outside the scope of this review. An introduction to the concepts involved and a comparison with other specific methods of teaching reading, such as i.t.a., can be found in the articles by Jones and Gattegno.

The use of some colour combinations can reduce the legibility of print. Thus, by using low brightness contrast between ink and paper or by using colour combinations unfamiliar or unattractive to the reader, poorer legibility can result. It is in this field that research studies have set down useful guidelines to be followed by printers. Where confusion exists in the research literature, is in the *nature of colour preferences* of children and adults and whether or not they are in conflict with measures of legibility. Investigation has centred around a child's preferences for warm shades over cool, high contrast over low, and naturalistic over unnaturalistic colour.

Tinker (1965, p. 237) states that *brightness contrast* between print and paper is perhaps the most important factor in the hygiene of vision. In experimental studies, speed of reading scores and perceptibility measures (of distance and exposure) correlated highly (+·86) and were related proportionally to the brightness contrast between print and paper. Tinker maintains on the basis of reader opinions that the stated preferred colours of readers and harmonizing colour combinations, can be used without sacrificing brightness contrast.

Relevant points made by Tinker concerning the legibility of colour, include:

i. the legibility of printed material does not depend primarily on the colour hues of the ink and paper as such, but on the contrast in brightness between them;

ii. brightness contrast is not the same thing as colour contrast. For example, dark red and blue have high hue contrast but little brightness contrast. Similarly, light orange and grey display saturation contrast, but have only slight brightness contrast. When printing with coloured ink on coloured paper for high legibility, the ink should be a shade (or dark colour) and the paper a tint (or light colour).

iii. attention should be given to the change in visual appearance of a colour when printed on a coloured background as opposed to printing on white. Tinker's experiment concerned coloured inks printed on coloured paper. The coloured effect is different when letters and background are both printed with differently coloured inks on a white paper so that they do not overlap.

Table 8 lists the relative legibility of print in 11 colour combinations

Sammy loved to be busy. He was never happier than when he was chuff-chuffing out of Derry Station on another trip to Uptown.

Three miles out of Derry the track climbed a steep hill, but Sammy knew how to take this part of the journey. 'Steady-and-slow!' he would say to himself as he went puff-puffing up the hill.

When he reached the top he would give a toot on his whistle, and go rushing down the other side, pretending that he was the Flying Scotsman. He loved to hear the clickety-click, clickety-click of the coaches hurrying along behind him.

Exactly on time he would pull into Uptown Station and come to a stop with a screech of brakes and a hiss of steam. The passengers all loved Sammy and often they would give him a friendly nod as they hurried past him towards the ticket-collector.

'Good old Sam,' they would say. 'Always on time is our Sammy.'

But now Sammy was feeling very sad. One Saturday morning the Station-master had come to visit him in his engine-shed. He began by praising Sammy, telling him how well he had done his work. He called Sammy 'a faithful servant'. And Sammy smiled rather sadly for he knew that the Station-master was bringing bad news.

The Station-master looked down at his boots. Then he said, 'Sammy, I have sad news for you. On Monday Danny the Diesel is coming to take over your run.'

And so on Saturday evening Sammy made his last trip to Derry, and on Monday he began to shunt the coaches and trucks in the station yard. He did not look up when Danny the Diesel drew out of Derry pulling the nine-five, Sammy's special run. He just kept his eyes on the track and let the steam sizzle sadly out of his chimney.

Day after day Sammy worked in the railway yard, pushing and shunting, but seldom getting a chance to go faster than three miles an hour—or maybe four.

His fine, shining, black paintwork soon became dirty and dull, so that even his friends, the Uptown passengers, sometimes did not recognise him.

Danny the Diesel was very popular. He could travel so fast and so smoothly. Because of this, more and more people began to travel on the Derry to Uptown line. Instead of four coaches Danny had to have five, then six, and sometimes seven. And there came a day when he was asked to pull eight coaches.

Sammy was just a little jealous when he saw Danny pulling smoothly out of Derry with eight fine new coaches packed with passengers.

The station yard was very quiet after Danny had gone. With a trickle of steam escaping from a little crack in his boiler Sammy dozed and later fell asleep. He was dreaming that he was racing the Flying Scotsman all the way to Edinburgh, when he awoke with a start. Someone was calling to him.

62375

(Tinker 1965, p. 163). A minus signifies less legibility than black on white.

TABLE 8: *Relative legibility of colour combinations*

Trade Name	Percentage of Difference in Legibility
Black on white	0·0
Grass green on white	−3·0
Lustre blue on white	−3·4
Black on yellow	−3·8
Tulip red on yellow	−4·8
Tulip red on white	−8·9
Grass green on red	−10·6
Chromium orange on black	−13·5
Chromium orange on white	−20·9
Tulip red on green	−39·5
Black on purple	−51·5

The first three colour combinations are only slightly less legible than black on white. The significant difference in legibility for tulip red on yellow suggests that it should not be used where speed of reading is important. The remaining colour combinations produce print which is almost illegible. Tinker recommends that 'the last four are so poor that it is inadvisable ever to use them'. Vickerstaff and Woolvin (1950) found with adult subjects that blue on white and green on white were preferred (significantly) to any other colour combinations tested. Readers' preferences were analysed and found to be based on the brightness contrast between ink and paper (even though the red ink was judged as bright as the blue or green, it ranked very low in readers' preferences). In an earlier experiment legibility was related to brightness contrast between ink and paper, but, contrary to Tinker's findings, only a slight connection was found to exist between legibility and the aesthetic appeal of colour combinations. Vickerstaff and Woolvin conclude by suggesting that legibility may be improved by *incorporating a pleasing colour contrast* (such as black on yellow) into the colour combination.

Child *et al.* (1968), in a study investigating the age and sex differences in children's colour preferences from grades 1 to 12, attempted to test the two commonly held beliefs that:

  i. children have hue preferences different from adults;
 ii. with increases in age children's preferences tend to shift from warm to cool colours.

In reviewing previous research literature, Child *et al.* found the results of developmental studies on colour preferences of children unconvincing. Where hue had been the intended variable in studies, it had often been confounded with value (brightness) and/or chroma (saturation). Subsequently, they controlled for differences in hue, value and chroma and measured the separate effect each had on colour preference. The results were analysed separately for the two sexes. Conclusions reached by Child *et al.* in this study, were as follows:

   i. Each dimension of colour experience can be considered individually as a determinant of preference.
  ii. A single set of simple laws cannot apply to changes in preference from childhood to adulthood; it is the interaction of dimensions that determines preference.
 iii. Children at all ages tend to prefer cooler colours, but at an early age hue is dominated by a preference for high chroma which suggests that highly saturated colours (which may be often warmer in hue) will be preferred to less saturated ones.
  iv. A general lessening of the childhood preference for high chroma, occurs with increases in age. This developmental trend may be related to the cognitive ability to differentiate and to experience.
   v. While some aspects of colour preference may differ a great deal from one society to another, the decrease in the relative influence of chroma with increases in age, remains a common trait.
  vi. Great differences were found to exist between colour preferences of boys and girls (e.g. girls preferred higher value to boys). However the general trend of colour preference was the same for the two sexes. Thus value (as preferred by both sexes) decreased with age.

Skoff and Pollack (1969) tested the visual acuity of children (age 7 to 14 years) as related to changes in colour (hue). Colours were matched for value and chroma. A saturation match for green could not be obtained which excluded green from the study. The colours tested were black, red, blue and yellow. The scores for yellow were not included in the results, due to the very low performance with yellow. (Subjects reported on the 'blurredness' of yellow which prevented discrimination of the colour stimulus.) The lowest visibility thresholds were obtained with black, followed by red, with blue the highest. This trend was consistent over the whole age range. The higher visual acuity of blue and red over black (especially of red over black) is in disagreement with most studies in this field. Skoff and Pollack did not use printed material in their experiment and this may account for the differences in scores. In experiments using printed material, the *familiarity of black on white* will always be a determining factor in its higher legibility over other colour combinations. The results of Skoff and Pollack may provide a more accurate measure of visual acuity in that they are not confounded by the past learning experiences of the subject. On the other hand they may have little practical application to the study of legibility as it concerns the printing of books.

Duthie (1971), in a study with children aged 11-17 years, found *high contrast within a configuration* the major factor determining colour preference. That is, high contrast along any, or all, of the three colour dimensions, was the 'key' to preference. Primary colours usually display high contrast, and as such were preferred by children. However, by adjusting the figure and background, a design of primary colours was devised with a contrast lower than an achromatic design. This resulted in a preference by the children for the achromatic design. In a subsequent study 19 art teachers and 19 adults (untrained in art) were tested by Duthie for colour preference. The preferences of the 19 adults were very similar to those shown by the children. In contrast, the scores of the art teachers were directly opposed to the preferences shown by the children and adults in the study. The distinct preference shown by art teachers for low contrast is in line with conclusions reached by

Child *et al.* (1968) who suggest that differences in cognitive development and past experience affect colour preferences. Designers, like art teachers, may be said to have a greater 'consciousness' of the dimensions of colour and may as a result perceive colour in a different context, to that of the general population.

Finally, consideration must be given to the practice of researchers to measure the responses of a subject to a *single stimulus*. Studies of this kind are artificial in that a subject very seldom responds to a single stimulus, especially in the normal reading situation. Of the many factors interacting to determine a subject's colour preference, the shape of the configuration is dominant. Duthie (1968) isolated two aspects of shape which he suggested influenced the legibility of the printed material as well as its aesthetic appeal. They were *symmetry* and *dispersion*. Duthie found that subjects were strongly influenced by the symmetry of a shape, tending to prefer a symmetric, rather than an asymmetric shape. A symmetric shape is also very legible. High dispersion on the other hand runs counter to standards of high visibility. The subjects' preference for high dispersion (where colours and shapes are less well differentiated) suggests that a configuration that attracts the most attention and is the most preferred by subjects, may be the least legible (as measured by its visual acuity).

B. The size, position and nature of illustrations

Magne and Parknas (1963, p. 266) described two functions of illustrations in books: information value and motivation value. Research studies are in general agreement as to the motivation value of illustrations in children's books. Vernon's comment (1953) that 'it is useless to expect younger children to study books without pictures' typifies the body of opinion held by most researchers in this field. Vernon, in the article 'The Value of Pictorial Illustration' (1953), notes that the motivational effect of pictorial material varies greatly with age, intelligence and education. The younger and less intelligent child gives more attention to illustrations than does the older, more sophisticated reader. The reading proficiency of the young child is so undeveloped that he is

Figure 19: *An example of a high information, low motivation illustration*

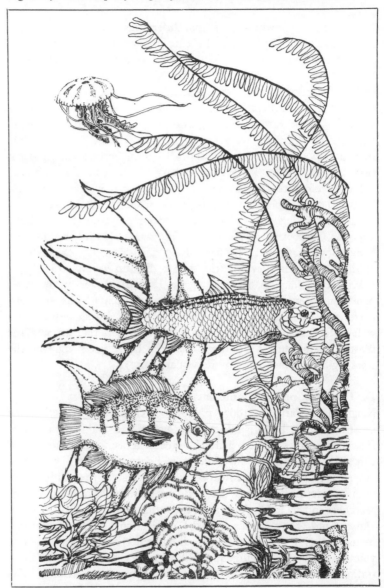

Figure 20: *An example of a low information, high motivation illustration*

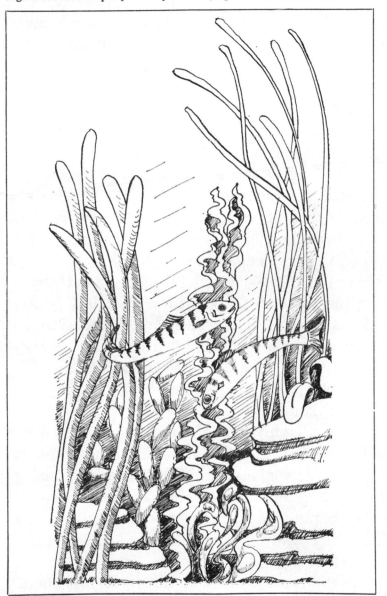

Sammy loved to be busy. He was never happier than when he was chuff-chuffing out of Derry Station on another trip to Uptown.

Three miles out of Derry the track climbed a steep hill, but Sammy knew how to take this part of the journey. ' Steady-and-slow ! ' he would say to himself as he went puff-puffing up the hill.

When he reached the top he would give a toot on his whistle, and go rushing down the other side, pretending that he was the Flying Scotsman. He loved to hear the clickety-click, clickety-click of the coaches hurrying along behind him.

Exactly on time he would pull into Uptown Station and come to a stop with a screech of brakes and a hiss of steam. The passengers all loved Sammy and often they would give him a friendly nod as they hurried past him towards the ticket-collector.

' Good old Sam,' they would say. ' Always on time is our Sammy.'

But now Sammy was feeling very sad. One Saturday morning the Station-master had come to visit him in his engine-shed. He began by praising Sammy, telling him how well he had done his work. He called Sammy ' a faithful servant '. And Sammy smiled rather sadly for he knew that the Station-master was bringing bad news.

The Station-master looked down at his boots. Then he said, ' Sammy, I have sad news for you. On Monday Danny the Diesel is coming to take over your run.'

And so on Saturday evening Sammy made his last trip to Derry, and on Monday he began to shunt the coaches and trucks in the station yard. He did not look up when Danny the Diesel drew out of Derry pulling the nine-five, Sammy's special run. He just kept his eyes on the track and let the steam sizzle sadly out of his chimney.

Day after day Sammy worked in the railway yard, pushing and shunting, but seldom getting a chance to go faster than three miles an hour—or maybe four.

His fine, shining, black paintwork soon became dirty and dull, so that even his friends, the Uptown passengers, sometimes did not recognise him.

Danny the Diesel was very popular. He could travel so fast and so smoothly. Because of this, more and more people began to travel on the Derry to Uptown line. Instead of four coaches Danny had to have five, then six, and sometimes seven. And there came a day when he was asked to pull eight coaches.

Sammy was just a little jealous when he saw Danny pulling smoothly out of Derry with eight fine new coaches packed with passengers.

The station yard was very quiet after Danny had gone. With a trickle of steam escaping from a little crack in his boiler Sammy dozed and later fell asleep. He was dreaming that he was racing the Flying Scotsman all the way to Edinburgh, when he awoke with a start. Someone was calling to him.

dependent on illustrations to gain meaning from the text and as an incentive to read the text. The older child who has some reading proficiency, will be sufficiently motivated to read if the context is of interest to him. Vernon postulates that in an uncontrolled situation, pictorial material might stimulate the reader to study a book or an article which he would otherwise ignore. Alternatively, pictures might encourage an active or thoughtful interest in the topic presented, whereas the verbal text alone would have left the reader unmoved.

The criticisms levelled at illustrations concern their ability to aid learning, i.e. their information value. Experimental studies have been carried out with primary and secondary school children using pictures as an accompaniment to verbal content (Vernon, 1953, 1954; Keir, 1970; Smith; and Watkins, 1972) and by presenting information pictorially (Magne and Parknas, 1963). In the latter method of pictorial representation, the motivation value of the illustration is regarded as being low compared to the high information value.

Vernon (1953) suggests that it is possible that illustrations may *detract from learning* by distracting attention from what the child is reading, causing him to remember the text less well. Vernon (1954) found that pictorial information had no significant effect on the recall of verbal material with 10- to 12-year-old subjects. Magne and Parknas (1963) found pictorial learning superior to verbal learning when retention was measured by both pictorial and verbal texts. No significant differences were found between the two methods of learning when retention was measured by verbal tests only. Smith and Watkins (1972) also used the two methods of testing retention of pictorial and verbal material. Unlike Magne and Parknas they found no significant differences in the scores between pictorial mode and verbal mode questions. The children using the illustrated material did better in both modes of questioning. This would tend to support Vernon's theory that an illustrated text provides greater motivation than an unillustrated text, resulting in greater attention being given to the text. In a comment on the article published by Magne and Parknas, Vernon (1964) attempts to clarify the discrepancy between research results by emphasizing the differences in the *nature* of the illustrated material. Pictures which are merely illustrations of what is clearly described in the text are said to be less useful as information transmitters than a pictorial representation of verbal information (as used by Magne and Parknas). Where children are required to remember the ideas or general gist of a text, rather than specific details, pictures may be distracting since they give too much emphasis to factual detail and too little to the general argument.

Smith and Watkins (1972), who used illustrations accompanying a text (in a similar manner as used by Vernon) found illustrations did aid learning. They attribute the lack of consistency in research results to the way in which the illustration is related to the verbal text. Illustrations that do little more than add interest value (such as those used by Vernon to show the production of a newspaper, facts about bridge constructions and docking of ships in harbour) may be distracting. However, illustrations that relate closely to text in such a way as to convey in a clear visual form the information and argument contained therein, should aid learning. The results obtained by Smith and Watkins in their 'Honeybee' experiment confirmed this assumption.

However, it may be argued that the significantly higher scores obtained by children using illustrated text, may have been due to the higher motivation value of the illustrations and not to their ability to transmit information. A better idea of the extent to which illustration can play in transmitting information would be gained if experimental material could be controlled for motivation value. The unillustrated Honeybee experimental material was unattractive to the young reader. The use of a highly attractive illustration (that is, one high in motivation value but low in information value) would provide a better measure of the part illustration plays in improving comprehension and retention of verbal material. Vernon (1954) maintains that a detailed and fully illustrative set of pictures may in themselves be no more effective than scattered and even slightly irrelevant pictures, in attracting attention, creating interest and enabling children to remember the general content of material. This hypothesis has yet to be tested experimentally.

Keir (1970) in an investigation (with seven- to eleven-year-olds) into the use of pictures as an aid to reading, stated that pictures by themselves may be of little value as information transmitters due to the inability of the child to recognize the content of the picture. Keir questions the commonly held belief that pictures aid learning (by linking the known to the unknown or by helping in general comprehension). Similarly, Vernon (1954) states that it 'seems clear that the child is not able by himself and without instruction to derive a coherent and meaningful pattern of information from illustrations'. Consequently, she maintains, pictures will have little effect in impressing upon the child concepts which to him have no logical coherence. This applies regardless of how interesting the pictures may make the text to the child. Keir takes this argument a stage further, emphasizing the need for teachers of young children to ensure that the child is aware of what the picture means. As this procedure may often defeat the purpose of the illustrations (e.g. illustrated dictionaries for independent work or books which children are motivated to read by themselves), it is important that publishers are aware of the ambiguity that may confront children, especially in the case of very common objects. Thus, for example, Keir states that children were unable to differentiate between lamb and sheep or goat, goose and turkey; other items also caused confusion and were named differently—jumper, pullover and sweater were used to name one illustration, van, lorry and truck another and string, wool and cotton a third. Some items in the illustrations detracted from the item to be named, for example, telegraph pole from electricity wires.

Other aspects investigated by Smith and Watkins (1972) included size and position of illustrations in relation to text, and the effective use of colour to enable children to derive maximum benefit from illustrations. Their study was carried out with primary school children from the ages of eight to eleven years. Among the important questions raised in the study were:

   i. Does the quest for variety and novelty in printing children's
      books, often leave little relationship between illustration and
      text?

Figure 22: *Examples of ambiguous illustrations*

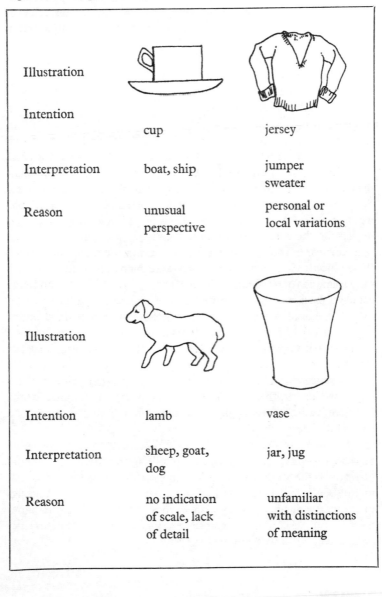

Illustration		
Intention	cup	jersey
Interpretation	boat, ship	jumper sweater
Reason	unusual perspective	personal or local variations
Illustration		
Intention	lamb	vase
Interpretation	sheep, goat, dog	jar, jug
Reason	no indication of scale, lack of detail	unfamiliar with distinctions of meaning

ii. If the relationship between text and illustration is vague, does the child ignore the illustration, or in his search for relevant illustration, is his reading interrupted and the information from the text lost or confused?

iii. Do children's own preferences for colour coincide with those attributed to them by publishers and parents?

iv. Does realism, both in colour and style of illustration, dominate a child's preferences?

Unfortunately, Smith and Watkins were unable to provide firm answers to these questions. Their test material and experimental design can be criticized for failure to control for many variables which may have influenced the children's preferences, independently of the variable being tested. Clearly the need to involve a designer in experiments of this kind is paramount. For example, children found a test card showing 'random' colouring of danger objects in the kitchen with non danger objects, more attractive than test cards showing systematic colouring (or failure to colour) these objects. Comprehension scores were higher for the systematically coloured (or uncoloured) cards. The preference for the randomly coloured card may be attributed to the symmetric pattern formed by the coloured objects compared to the scattered pattern of the other test card. The colouring (dark red) also tended to interfere with the structure of many of the danger objects, making them less attractive to the child, e.g. the electric radiator and steam from boiling saucepan. This was not the case for the 'non danger' items (e.g. curtains, mother's skirt, child's clothing). A designer would be more aware of these inconsistencies in the test material and control for them accordingly.

Research studies have not, to date, been able to supply answers to the questions raised by Smith and Watkins. Reference should be made to the studies in part A of this section on the use of colour in children's books, as they indicate the nature of current findings in this particular field. They also serve to emphasize the difficulties involved in designing an experiment that is able to measure accurately the variable being tested.

SECTION FIVE

Summary

IT HAS NOT been possible, from an examination of the research literature, to set down a 'list of rules' to be followed by publishers in the printing of children's books. Nor has it been possible to state categorically what is *totally unacceptable* in the printing of books for children, in preference to *degrees of what might be regarded as acceptable*. For the majority of typographic factors discussed in this report, there exists *a range* of conditions which provide for acceptable standards of legibility. Within this range there are recommended optima and possible thresholds, below which identification of the print becomes difficult. For example, 10 point to 14 point type size is satisfactory for adult readers. Eleven point is the optimum recommended by Tinker for greatest ease and speed of reading while eight point is the smallest size recommended for reading of continuous prose. One reason suggested for the inability to arrive at precise standards of optimal legibility, is the effect psychological factors have on measures of legibility. Thus research studies emphasize the part played by customary reading habits, by familiarity with the printed material and by the idiosyncratic nature of personal preferences and attitudes towards the printed material. It is only by a greater awareness of the nature of these psychological factors, that the results obtained from research studies in typography can be placed in their correct perspective and thus have some practical application to the printing of children's books.

Children today live in a social environment where large quantities of accessible material in the form of newspapers, comic books, magazines, books and television, help in creating attitudes towards reading. One may ask is there a need for a 'learn to read' series of

Sammy loved to be busy. He was never happier than when he was chuff-chuffing out of Derry Station on another trip to Uptown.

Three miles out of Derry the track climbed a steep hill, but Sammy knew how to take this part of the journey. ' Steady-and-slow ! ' he would say to himself as he went puff-puffing up the hill.

When he reached the top he would give a toot on his whistle, and go rushing down the other side, pretending that he was the Flying Scotsman. ' He loved to hear the clickety-click, clickety-click of the coaches hurrying along behind him.

Exactly on time he would pull into Uptown Station and come to a stop with a screech of brakes and a hiss of steam. The passengers all loved Sammy and often they would give him a friendly nod as they hurried past him towards the ticket-collector.

' Good old Sam,' they would say. ' Always on time is our Sammy.'

But now Sammy was feeling very sad. One Saturday morning the Station-master had come to visit him in his engine-shed. He began by praising Sammy, telling him how well he had done his work. He called Sammy ' a faithful servant '. And Sammy smiled rather sadly for he knew that the Station-master was bringing bad news.

The Station-master looked down at his boots. Then he said, ' Sammy, I have sad news for you. On Monday Danny the Diesel is coming to take over your run.'

And so on Saturday evening Sammy made his last trip to Derry, and on Monday he began to shunt the coaches and trucks in the station yard. He did not look up when Danny the Diesel drew out of Derry pulling the nine-five, Sammy's special run. He just kept his eyes on the track and let the steam sizzle sadly out of his chimney.

Day after day Sammy worked in the railway yard, pushing and shunting, but seldom getting a chance to go faster than three miles an hour—or maybe four.

His fine, shining, black paintwork soon became dirty and dull, so that even his friends, the Uptown passengers, sometimes did not recognise him.

Danny the Diesel was very popular. He could travel so fast and so smoothly. Because of this, more and more people began to travel on the Derry to Uptown line. Instead of four coaches Danny had to have five, then six, and sometimes seven. And there came a day when he was asked to pull eight coaches.

Sammy was just a little jealous when he saw Danny pulling smoothly out of Derry with eight fine new coaches packed with passengers.

The station yard was very quiet after Danny had gone. With a trickle of steam escaping from a little crack in his boiler Sammy dozed and later fell asleep. He was dreaming that he was racing the Flying Scotsman all the way to Edinburgh, when he awoke with a start. Someone was calling to him.

books, which becomes separated in the child's mind, from the
books the child likes to have read to him and which he conceives
as being 'real books'? Would it not be preferable to combine these
two functions (educational and motivational) in a book that creates
an attitude towards learning to read that is related to the home and
society, rather than to the school room?

Perhaps the most important points to emerge from the study
of the research material are as follows:

i. Reader attitudes and motivation towards the printed material
   are more important than typographic factors in measures of
   legibility.

ii. Within this context, a vast amount of work has been done which
    is not well enough known to teachers or publishers—or even
    to other researchers. Although the research literature does not
    supply ready made answers to publisher's questions, those
    responsible for publishing children's books would be helped
    greatly by knowledge of its findings.

iii. 'Rules' of legibility for beginning readers are not the same as
     those for experienced readers.

To compile a list of DO'S and DONT'S would require further
research into some of the areas highlighted in this report. Research
on legibility can, however, become lost in the minutiae of experimental manipulations. The dilemma is best illustrated by a
quotation from Hartley and Mills (1973):

'Typographical research is remarkable for its number of variables,
all of which can be manipulated and all of which interact. Jaspert
et al. (1970) reported 2,327 (such variables). . . . It is perhaps
not surprising therefore that much typographical decision-
making is implicit rather than explicit, and that there are demands
for new, and more rational approaches to typography.'

Glossary

ACHROMATIC	Free from colour.
ASCENDER	That part of a lower case letter which rises above the x-height, as in b, d, f, h, k, l.
ASTIGMATISM	Structural defect in the eye, preventing correct focussing.
CHROMATIC	Full of bright colour.
DESCENDER	That part of a lower case letter which descends below the base line, as in j, p, q, y.
DYSLEXIA	Perceptual and linguistic handicaps which result in reading and writing disabilities.
EM	The square of the body of any size of type. Derived from the letter M, whose capital, the widest of the fount, occupies the whole body width.
FOUNT or font	Complete set of a particular size and design of type comprising lower case, capitals, small capitals, figures and punctuation marks.
HANGING numerals	Numerals with ascenders and descenders above and below x-height of type. Found in all old type faces.
INVARIANT feature	Those features of a letter or object which remain substantially the same despite minor variations (e.g. rotations) in the whole configuration in which they are contained.
IRRADIATION	Apparent extension of edges of illuminated object against a dark ground.

LEADING	Extra space between lines of type.
MYOPIA	Short sightedness.
LEGIBILITY	The ease and accuracy with which meaningful printed material is comprehended.
LOWER CASE	Small letters in a fount (a, b, c, etc.) as opposed to capitals and small capitals.
PERCEPTIBILITY	Distance of perception of a visual stimulus.
PICA	The printer's measurement of a line length; one pica equals 12 points; 12 points equals approximately one sixth of an inch.
POINT SIZE	The printer's basic unit of measurement of type size, equal to 1/72 inch, or 72 points equal approximately one inch.
RANGING or lining numerals	Numerals of uniform height found in modern type faces.
SANS SERIF	A style of type which has no serifs.
SERIF	The finishing strokes at the top and bottom of a letter.
SOLID SETTING	Type set without extra spacing or leading.
TACHISTOSCOPE	An instrument which permits perception of a visual stimulus under controlled conditions of exposure.
TYPEFACE	The style or design of a particular type fount. Examples used in this report include Gill Medium, Modern 7, Grotesque 215, Univers, Spartan, Scotch Roman, Times Roman and Air Force Fount.
UPPERCASE	Capital letters e.g. A, B, C.
VISUAL ACUITY	The sharpness or clearness of vision.
WEIGHT or boldness	The degree of heaviness of a typeface e.g. light, medium or **bold.**
X - HEIGHT	The height of lower case letters without ascenders and descenders, as measured from the base line to the top of the face of the lower case x.

Figure 24: *Typographical dimensions*

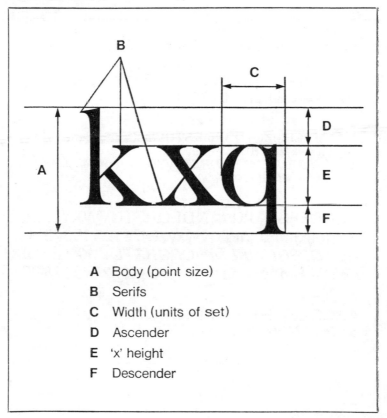

A Body (point size)
B Serifs
C Width (units of set)
D Ascender
E 'x' height
F Descender

Figure 25: *Gill Sans, Grotesque No. 1, Univers Medium and Spartan Light founts*

ABCDEFGHIJKLMNOPQRSTUVWXYZabcdefghij
klmnopqrstuvwxyz&!?£1234567890
ABCDEFGHIJKLMNOPQRSTUVWXYZabcdefghijklmno
pqrstuvwxyz&!?£1234567890

ABCDEFGHIJKLMNOPQRSTUVWXYZabcdefghijklmn
opqrstuvwxyz&!?£1234567890
ABCDEFGHIJKLMNOPQRSTUVWXYZabcdefghijklmnop
qrstuvwxyz &!?£1234567890

ABCDEFGHIJKLMNOPQRSTUVWXYZabc
defghijklmnopqrstuvwxyz&!?£1234567890
ABCDEFGHIJKLMNOPQRSTUVWXYZabc
defghijklmnopqrstuvwxyz&!?£1234567890

ABCDEFGHIJKLMNOPQRSTUVWXYZ
&!?£1234567890

Figure 26: *Scotch Roman, Modern No. 7 and Monotype No. 8 founts*

ABCDEFGHIJKLMNOPQRSTUVWXY
ZÆŒ& £ abcdefghijklmnopqrstuvwxyz
æœ fiffflffiffl 1234567890 *ABCDEFGHI*
JKLMNOPQRSTUVWXYZÆŒ& abcd
efghijklmnopqrstuvwxyzæœ :;!? fiffflffiffl"()[]
ABCDEFGHIJKLMNOPQRSTUVWXYZÆŒ .,:;-!?

ABCDEFGHIJKLMNOPQRSTUVWXYZ
ÆŒ& £ abcdefghijklmnopqrstuvwxyzæœ
fiffflffiffl 1234567890 *ABCDEFGHIJKLM*
NOPQRSTUVWXYZÆŒ& abcdefghijklm
nopqrstuvwxyzæœ :;!? fiffflffiffl ABCDEFGH
IJKLMNOPQRSTUVWXYZÆŒ .,:;-!?"()[]

ABCDEFGHIJKLMNOPQRSTUVWXYZ Æ
Œ& £ abcdefghijklmnopqrstuvwxyzæœ fiffflffi
ffl 1234567890 *ABCDEFGHIJKLMNOPQR*
STUVWXYZÆŒ& abcdefghijklmnopqrstuvw
xyzæœ :;!? fiffflffiffl ABCDEFGHIJKLMNOPQRST
UVWXYZÆŒ .,:;-!?"()[]

Introductory Guide to the Research Literature

The following texts provide an introduction to the research literature on the legibility of print and the reading process.

BUCKINGHAM, B. R. (1931)

New Data on the Typography of Text-books.

An example of a systematic experimental design, applied to a substantial sample of children (2,010) at an early stage in learning to read. Buckingham investigates the effects of variations in size of type, length of line and leading, on speed of reading and comprehension scores.

BURT, C. (1959)

A Psychological Study of Typography.

This investigation, undertaken as a contribution to psychology rather than typography, provides insight into problems of experimental design, by emphasizing the influence of psychological factors on measurements of legibility. Poor documentation throughout the text reduces the effectiveness of much of the material—31 references.

CARMICHAEL, L. and DEARBORN, W. F. (1972: 2nd ed.)

Reading and Visual Fatigue.

First edition published in 1947. Authors report on extensive studies made to discover whether visual fatigue could be used as a measure of legibility. Detailed descriptions are given of the photographic devices used to measure eye movements. A well documented text—409 references.

FOSTER, J. J.
(1972)

Legibility Research Abstracts 1971.
A second issue of a publication which sets out to assist graphic designers to keep up with the technical literature relevant to their subject. Contains 332 abstracts obtained from 57 periodicals which are mainly psychological, but some scientific and technical titles are included. Abstracts mainly concern the physical characteristics of the message and the effect of reading conditions on the reader's response. Related fields, such as the relationship between perceptual abilities and reading performance and the comparison of reading with other methods of communication, are included to a lesser extent.

HUEY, E. B.
(1968: 2nd ed.)

The Psychology and Pedagogy of Reading.
First edition was published in 1908 and is regarded as a classic text in the study of reading. Huey discusses the nature of the perceptual processes involved in reading and relates these to the printed material and to teaching methods. The text is well documented throughout.

MELNIK, A. and
MERRITT, J.
(1972)

Reading Today and Tomorrow.
A book of articles edited by the Reading Development course team at the Open

D

University. Articles include those on
the nature of reading, media and the
reader, reading development and the
future of reading. Authors include
J. Downing, K. S. Goodman, E. J.
Goodacre, J. F. Reid and N. B. Smith.

SMITH, F.   *Understanding Reading: A Psycho-*
(1971)   *linguistic Analysis of Reading and*
                 Learning to Read.
                 Provides an analysis of the reading
                 process, distinguishing between letter,
                 word and meaning identification. Also
                 considers types of learning, the struc-
                 ture of the visual system, eye move-
                 ments, teaching reading, linguistics and
                 the relationship between speech and
                 reading.

SPENCER, H.   *The Visible Word.*
(1969)   Contains a detailed review of the
                 research literature on legibility of
                 typography with special emphasis on
                 the changes in printing techniques
                 required in an age of electronics and
                 multi-media systems of communica-
                 tion. A very well illustrated and well
                 documented text—464 references.

TINKER, M. A.   *Bases for Effective Reading.*
(1965)   A well co-ordinated exposition of avail-
                 able information on the reading process.
                 Includes discussion of the nature of
                 reading, perception, comprehension and
                 eye movements. These are related to
                 research findings on the legibility of

typography and other factors such as illumination which affect the ease and proficiency of reading—356 references. *Legibility of Print* (1963) by Tinker is also recommended.

VERNON, M.
(1971)

Reading and its Difficulties.
Replaces author's earlier book *Backwardness in Reading* (1957). Emphasis is on the visual, linguistic and motivational aspects of reading as they affect the normal and handicapped child. Very well documented—409 references.

ZACHRISSON, B.
(1965)

Legibility of Printed Text.
Emphasis more on research studies carried out in Europe, especially in Sweden, which makes the book a valuable addition to the research literature. Detailed treatment is given to problems of definition and measurement of legibility in experimental situations. Other important sections include aesthetic considerations and the effect familiarity of material has on experimental findings—240 references.

Bibliography

BALLANTINE, F. A. (1951). *Age Changes in Measures of Eye Movements in Silent Reading*. Ann Arbor, Michigan: Univ. of Michigan Press (Univ. of Michigan Monographs in Education, No. 4).

BAMBERGER, R. (1972). *Bridging the Gap Between Children's Book People and Reading People*. United Kingdom Reading Association.

BLACKHURST, J. H. (1927). *Investigations in the Hygiene of Reading*. Baltimore: Warwick and York.

BERGER, C. (1948). 'Some experiments on the width of symbols as determinant of legibility', *Acta Ophthalmologica*, 26, 517–50.

BERGER, C. (1959). 'Measurement, definition and unit of legibility', *Die Farbe*, 8, 29–32.

BIEMILLER, A. (1970). 'The development of the use of graphic and contextual information as children learn to read', *Reading Research Quarterly*, 6, 75–96.

BOUMA, H. (1971), 'Visual recognition of isolated lower case letters', *Vision Research*, 11, 459–74.

BRITISH ASSOCIATION FOR THE ADVANCEMENT OF SCIENCE (1913). *Report of Committee on the Influence of Schoolbooks upon Eyesight*. London: Murray.

BUCKINGHAM, B. R. (1931). *New Data on the Typography of Textbooks*. 30th Yearbook. Part II of the National Society for Study of Education, Chicago. University of Chicago Press, 93–125.

BURT, C. (1959). *A Psychological Study of Typography*. London: CUP.

BURT, C. (1960). 'The typography of children's books—a record of research in the UK', in: *Yearbook of Education*, 242–56.

BUSWELL, G. T. (1937). *Fundamental Reading Habits: a Study of their Development*. Chicago: University of Chicago Press.

CALDWELL, E. C. and HALL, V. O. (1970). 'Distinctive features versus prototype learning re-examined', *J. Exper. Psychol.*, 83, 7.

CARMICHAEL, L. and DEARBORN, W. F. (1972). *Reading and Visual Fatigue*. Connecticut: Greenwood. (Original edition, 1947. Boston: Houghton Mifflin.)

CARRILLO, L. W. (1972). 'Developing flexibility of reading rate', in CLARK and MILNE (Eds.), *Reading and Related Skills*. London: Ward Lock Educational.

CHALL, J. (1967). *Learning to Read: The Great Debate*. Maidenhead: McGraw-Hill.

CHILD, I. L., HANSEN, J. A. and HORNBECK, F. W. (1968). 'Age and sex differences in children's colour preferences', *Child Development*, 39, I, 237–47.

CLARK, M. and MILNE, A. (1972). *Reading and Related Skills*. Proceedings of the 9th annual study conference of UKRA. London: Ward Lock Educational.

CLAY, M. (1968). *Emergent Reading Behaviour*. Reviewed by S. WEINTRAUB in the *Reading Teacher*, 22, 63–7.

COLEMAN, E. B. and HAHN, S. C. (1966). 'Failure to improve readability with a vertical typography', *J. Appl. Psychol.*, 50, 434–6.

CROSLAND, H. R. and JOHNSON, G. (1928). 'The range of apprehension as affected by interletter hair spacing and by the characteristics of individual letters', *J. Appl. Psychol.*, XII, 82.

D'ARCY, P. (1973). *Reading for Meaning 2: The Reader's Response*. London: Hutchinson Educational.

DOWNING, J. (1969). 'How children think about reading', *The Reading Teacher*, 23, III, 217–30.

DUNN-RANKIN, P. (1968). 'The similarity of lower case letters of the English alphabet', *J. Verbal Learning Behaviour*, 1, 990.

DUTHIE, R. K. (1968). 'Contrast as a measure of complexity and its effect on children's preferences for colour complexes'. Unpublished research study.

DUTHIE, R. K. (1971). 'Colour contrast and its effect on preference', *Colour Review*, Autumn 1971, 12–13.

FABRIZIO, R., KAPLAN, I. and TEAL, G. (1967). 'Readability as a function of the straightness of the R-hand margins', *J. Typographic Res.*, 1, 90–5.

FISHER, V. L. and PRICE, J. H. (1970). 'Cues to word similarity used by children and adults: supplementary report', *Percep. and Motor Skills*, 31, 849–50.

FLORES, I. (1960). 'Methods of comparing the legibility of printed numerals', *J. Psychol.*, 50, 3–14.

FOSTER, J. J. (1972). *Legibility Research Abstracts, 1971*. London: Lund Humphries.

GALOCY, T. C. (1970). 'The effects of pre-training in transfer letter naming on the rate children learn', *Dissertation Abstracts International*, 30, 12, 5339A–5340A.

GATTEGNO, C. (1962). *Words in Colour Reading*. Educational Explorers.

GIBSON, E. J., GIBSON, J. J., PICK, A. D. and OSSER, H. (1962). 'A developmental study of the discrimination of letter-like forms', *J. Comp. Physiol. Psychol.*, 55, 897–906.

GIBSON, E. J. (1965). 'Learning to read', *Science*, 148, 1066.

GILLILAND, J. (1972). *Readability*. London: University of London Press.

GOODACRE, E. J. (1967). *Reading in Infant Classes*. Slough: NFER.

GOODMAN, K. S. (1967). 'Reading: a psycholinguistic guessing game', *J. Reading Specialist*, May, 1967.

HARTLEY, J. and MILLS, R. L. (1973). 'Unjustified experiments in typography', *Brit. J. Educ. Technol.*, 2.

HODGE, D. C. (1962). 'Legibility of uniform stroke-width alphabet', *J. Engineering Psychol.*, 2, 55–67.

HOLDEN, M. H. and MACGINITIE, W. H. (1972). 'Children's conceptions of word boundaries in speech and print', *J. Educ. Psychol.*, 63, 6, 551–7.

HORTON, D. L. and MERCHERIKOFF, M. (1960). 'Letter preferences: ranking of the alphabet', *J. Appl. Psychol.*, 44, 252–3.

HOVDE, H. T. (1930). 'The relative effects of size of type, leading and context', *J. Appl. Psychol.*, 14, 63–73.

HUEY, E. B. (1908). *The Psychology and Pedagogy of Reading.* New York: Macmillan/MIT Press.

JASPERT, W. P., BERRY, W. T. and JOHNSON, A. F. (1970). *The Encyclopaedia of Typefaces* (4th ed.). London: Blandford.

JONES, J. K. (1967). 'Interim Results in the Colour Story Reading Experiment', in: DANIELS, J. C. (Ed.), *Reading Problems and Perspectives* (Report of Reading Study Conference, Nottingham, 1967). UK Reading Association.

JONES, J. K. (1968). 'Comparing i.t.a. with colour story reading', *Educ. Res.*, 10, 226.

KERR, J. (1926). *The Fundamentals of School Health.* London: Allen and Unwin.

KEIR, G. (1970). 'The use of pictures as an aid to reading', *Reading*, 4, 6–11.

KLARE, G. R., MABRY, J. E. and GUSTAFSON, L. M. (1955). 'The relationship of human interest to immediate retention and to acceptability of technical material', *J. Appl. Psychol.*, 39, 92–5.

KLARE, G. R., MABRY, J. E. and GUSTAFSON, L. M. (1955). 'The relationship of patterning (underlining) to immediate retention and to acceptability of technical material', *J. Appl. Psychol.*, 39, 40–2.

KLARE, G. R., SHUFORD, E. H. and NICHOLS, W. H. (1957). 'Relationship of style difficulty, practice and ability to efficiency of reading and retention', *J. Appl. Psychol.*, 41, 222–6.

KLARE, G. K., SHUFORD, E. H. and NICHOLS, W. H. (1958). 'The relation of format organization to learning', *Educ. Res. Bull.*, 37, 39–45.

KOLERS, P. A. (1969). 'Reading is only incidentally visual', in GOODMAN, K. S. and FLEMING, J. T. (Eds.), *Psycholinguistics and the Teaching of Reading.* International Reading Association.

LETSON, C. T. (1958). 'Speed and comprehension in reading', *J. Educ. Res.*, 52, 49–53.

LUCKIESH, M. and MOSS, F. K. (1938). 'Visibility and readability of print on white and tinted papers', *Sight Saving Review*, 8, 123–34.

LUCKIESH, M. and MOSS, F. K. (1940). 'Boldness as a factor in type design and typography', *J. Appl. Psychol.*, 24, 170–83.

LUCKIESH, M. and MOSS, F. K. (1940). 'Criterion of readability', *J. Exper. Psychol.*, 27, 256–70.

MAGNE, O. and PARKNAS, L. (1963). 'Learning effects of pictures', *Brit. J. Educ. Psychol.*, 33, 265–75.

MELNIK, A. and MERRITT, J. (1972). *Reading: Today and Tomorrow.* London: University of London Press.

MCNAMARA, W. G., PATERSON, D. G. and TINKER, M. A. (1953). 'The influence of size of type on speed of reading in primary grades', *Sight Saving Review*, 23, 28.

MOSLEY, J. (1965). 'The Nymph and the Grot. The revival of the sanserif letter', *Typographica*, 12, 2–19.

NEISSER, U. (1963). 'The multiplicity of thought', *Brit. J. Psychol.*, 54, 1.

OVINK, G. W. (1938). See ZACHRISSON, 1965.

PATERSON, D. G. and TINKER, M. A. (1929). 'Studies of typographical factors influencing speed of reading', *J. Appl. Psychol.*, XIII, 120–30, 205–19.

PATERSON, D. G. and TINKER, M. A. (1932). 'Studies of typographical factors influencing speed of reading', *J. Appl. Psychol.*, XVI, 605–13.

PATERSON, D. G. and TINKER, M. A. (1940). *How to Make Type Readable.* New York: Harper and Row.

PATERSON, D. G. and TINKER, M. A. (1940). 'Influence of line width on eye movements', *J. Exper. Psychol.*, 27, 572–7.

PAYNE, D. E. (1967). 'Readability of typewritten material: proportional versus standard spacing', *J. Typographic Res.*, 1, 125–36.

PIAGET, J. and INHELDER, B. (1956). *The Child's Conception of Space.* London: Routledge and Kegan Paul.

PITMAN, I. J. (1961). *Learning to Read.* London: Royal Society of Arts.

POPP, H. M. (1964). 'Visual discrimination of alphabet letters', *The Reading Teacher*, 17, 221–6.

POULTON, E. C. (1965). 'Letter differentiation and rate of comprehension in reading', *J. Appl. Psychol.*, 49, 5, 358–62.

PRINCE, J. H. (1967). 'Printing for the visually handicapped', *J. Typographic Res.*, 1, 31–47.

PYKE, R. L. (1926). *Report on the Legibility of Print.* London: HMSO.

REID, J. (1966). 'Learning to think about reading', *Educ. Res.*, 9, 56–62.

ROETHLEIN, B. E. (1912). 'The relative legibility of different faces of printing types', *Amer. J. Psychol.*, 23, 1–36.

SCHONELL, F. J. (1945). *The Psychology and Teaching of Reading.* Edinburgh: Oliver and Boyd.

SHAW, A. (1969). *Print for a Partial Sight—a Research Report.* London Library Association.

SHAW, E. R. (1902). *School Hygiene.* London: Macmillan.

SKOFF, E. and POLLACK, R. H. (1969). 'Visual acuity in children as a function of hue', *Perception and Psychophysics*, 6 (4), 244–6.

SMITH, F. (1971). *Understanding Reading.* New York: Holt Rinehart & Winston.

SMITH, J. and WATKINS, H. (1972). 'An investigation into some aspects of the illustration of primary school books'. Typography Unit, Univ. of Reading.

SMITH, N. B. (1928). 'Matching ability as a factor in first-grade reading', *J. Educ. Psychol.*, 19, 560–71.

SMYTHE, P. C., STENNETT, R. G., HARDY, M., and WILSON, H. R. (1971). 'Knowledge of upper case and lower case names', *J. Reading Behaviour*, 3, 24–33.

SMYTHE, P. C., STENNETT, R. G., HARDY, M. and WILSON, H. R. (1971). 'Visual discrimination of primary type upper case and lowei case letters', *J. Reading Behaviour*, 3, 6–13.

SOAR, R. S. (1955). 'Height-width proportion and stroke width in numerical visibility', *J. Appl. Psych.*, 39, 43–6.

SPENCER, H. (1969). *The Visible Word.* London: Lund Humphries.

STANTON, F. N. and BURTT, H. E. (1935). 'The influence of surface and tint of paper on the speed of reading', *J. Appl. Psychol.*, 19, 683–93.

TAYLOR, C. D. (1934). 'The relative legibility of black and white print', *J. Educ. Psychol.*, 25, 561–78.

TINKER, M. A. (1928). 'The relative legibility of the letters, digits and of certain mathematical signs', *J. General Psychol.*, 1, 472–96.

TINKER, M. A. (1930). 'The relative legibility of modern and old style numerals', *J. Exper. Psychol.*, 13, 453–61.

TINKER, M. A. (1932). 'The effect of colour on visual apprehension and perception', *Genet. Psychol. Mon.*, 11, 61–136.

TINKER, M. A. (1932). 'The influence of form of type on the perception of words', *J. Appl. Psychol.*, 16, 167–74.

TINKER, M. A. (1943). 'Readability of comic books', *Amer. J. Optometry*, 20, 89–93.

TINKER, M. A. (1955). 'Prolonged reading tasks in visual research', *J. Appl. Psychol.*, 39, 6, 414.

TINKER, M. A. (1956). 'Effects of sloped text upon the readability of print', *Amer. J. Optometry*, 33, 189–95.

TINKER, M. A. (1959). 'Print for children's textbooks', *Education* (USA), 80, 1, 37–40.

TINKER, M. A. (1963). 'Legibility of print for children in the upper grades', *Amer. J. Optom. and Arch. Amer. Acad. Optometry*, 40, 614–21.

TINKER, M. A. (1963). *Legibility of Print*. Ames: Iowa State Univ. Press.

TINKER, M. A. (1965). *Bases for Effective Reading*. Ames: Iowa State Univ. Press.

TINKER, M. A. and PATERSON, D. G. (1942). 'Reader preferences and typography', *J. Appl. Psychol.*, 26, 38–40.

TINKER, M. A. and PATERSON, D. G. (1946). 'Readability of mixed type forms', *J. Appl. Psychol.*, 30, 631–7.

VERNON, M. D. (1929). *Studies in the Psychology of Reading*. London: HMSO, 5–36.

VERNON, M. D. (1953). 'The value of pictorial illustration', *Brit. J. Educ. Psychol.*, 23, 180–7.

VERNON, M. D. (1954). 'The instruction of children by pictorial illustration', *Brit. J. Educ. Psychol.*, 24, 171–9.

VERNON, M. D. (1964). 'Comment on article by Magne and Parknas', *Brit. J. Educ. Psychol.*, 34, 204.

VERNON, M. D. (1971). *Reading and Its Difficulties*. Cambridge: Cambridge University Press.

VICKERSTAFF, T. and WOOLVIN, C. S. (1950). 'Investigation of the legibility and aesthetic value of coloured printing inks on coloured papers', *Colour*, ICI.

WEBSTER, J. (1965). *Practical Reading*. London: Evans Brothers.

WILLIAMS, J. P., BLUMBERG, E. L. and WILLIAMS, D. V. (1970). *Cues Used in Visual Word Recognition*, in FOSTER, J. J., *Legibility Research Abstracts, 1971*. London: Lund Humphries.

WROLSTAD, M. E. (1960). 'Adult preferences in typography: exploring the function of design', *Journalism Quarterly*, 37, 211–23.

ZACHRISSON, B. (1957). *Studies in the Readability of Printed Text with Special Reference to Type Design and Type Size*. Stockholm: Graphic Institute.

ZACHRISSON, B. (1965). *Legibility of Printed Text*. Stockholm: Graphic Institute.